Great Monologues for Young Actors

. . .

VOLUME III

SMITH AND KRAUS PUBLISHERS
MONOLOGUE ANTHOLOGIES FOR YOUNG ACTORS

Winners Competition Series Volume 1: Award-winning 60-Second Monologues for Ages 5-12 by Janet Milstein

Winners Competition Series Volume 3: Award-winning 60-Second Monologues for Ages 13-18 by Janet Milstein

Great Monologues for Young Actors Volumes 1 and 2

Teens Speak: 60 Original Character Monologues for Girls Ages 13-15

Teens Speak: 60 Original Character Monologues for Boys Ages 13-15

Teens Speak: 60 Original Character Monologues for Girls Ages 16-18

Teens Speak: 60 Original Character Monologues for Boys Ages 16-18

Multicultural Monologues for Young Actors

Monologues in Dialect for Young Actors

The Spirit of America: Patriotic Monologues and Speeches for Middle and High School Students

Hot Spots for Teens Volume 1: One-Person Cold-reading Copy for TV Commercial Audition Success

The Ultimate Audition Book for Teens Volume 1: 111 One-Minute Monologues

The Ultimate Audition Book for Teens Volume 2: 111 One-Minute Monologues

The Ultimate Audition Book for Teens Volume 3: 111 One-Minute Monologues

The Ultimate Audition Book for Teens Volume 4: 111 One-Minute Monologues

The Ultimate Audition Book for Teens Volume 5: 111 Shakespeare Monologues

The Ultimate Audition Book for Teens Volume 6: 111 One-Minute Monologues for Teens by Teens

The Ultimate Audition Book for Teens Volume 7: 111 Monologues from Classical Theater, 2 Minutes and Under

The Ultimate Audition Book for Teens Volume 9: 111 Monologues from Contemporary Literature, 2 Minutes and Under

The Ultimate Audition Book for Teens Volume 10: 111 One-Minute Monologues for Teens by Teens

The Ultimate Audition Book for Teens Volume 11: One-Minute Monologues by Type

The Ultimate Audition Book for Teens Volume 12: 111 One-Minute Monologues — Just Comedy!

The Ultimate Audition Book for Teens Volume 13: 111 One-Minute Monologues — Active Voices

To order call toll-free (888) 282-2881

for more information visit us online at www.smithandkraus.com

Great Monologues
for Young Actors

. . .

VOLUME III

Edited by
Craig Slaight and Jack Sharrar

YOUNG ACTORS SERIES

A Smith and Kraus Book

A Smith and Kraus Book
Published by Smith and Kraus, Inc.
Hanover, New Hampshire 03755
www.smithandkraus.com / (888) 282-2881

First Edition: November 2008
10 9 8 7 6 5 4 3 2 1

The Young Actors Series
ISBN-13 978-1-57525-408-1 / ISBN-10 1-57525-408-5
LIBRARY OF CONGRESS CONTROL NUMBER: 2008935714

NOTE: These monologues are intended to be used for audition and class study; permission is not required to use the material for those purposes. However, if there is a paid performance of any of the monologues included in this book, please refer to the Rights and Permissions pages 181–183 to locate the source that can grant permission for public performance.

Contents

• • •

Monologues for Young Women

Monologues for Young Men

Song Lyrics as Monologues

Lyrics by Bob Dylan

Introduction
The Monologue Audition

• • •

[Note: Although many of the speeches in this book are appropriate for auditions, not all the material in this collection will be suitable for auditions. Some selections are meant for study and exploration in acting techniques. In any audition situation, the first thing to ascertain is what is required. You must carefully seek the exact nature of the audition before selecting material.]

As professional directors who work at a major American regional theater, and acting teachers who have been teaching young and journeymen actors for many years, we often find auditions lacking the central preparation necessary to make them successful. We can all agree that auditions may not be the most effective way to assess acting potential. However, until another method has been introduced, we are all (actors and directors) saddled with the standard two-minute meeting. Here are some of the areas of challenge in auditioning with monologues.

What material should I pick?
The most useful advice here is to select material spoken by characters that you could believably play. If your audition is for a specific role in a particular play, listen carefully for what is required for the audition. If the director/producer wishes to hear you in a speech of your choosing, select something of a similar tone to the play for which you are auditioning. Unless required, don't use a speech from the play for which you are auditioning. Because roles are created in an evolutionary process during rehearsals, with much input from the director (or the writer if it is a new play), why lay out impressions

before you've had the opportunity to discuss and work on the role with the director unless you absolutely have to? If you are doing a general audition (for the purpose of ascertaining an overall impression of your work as an actor), again your choices should be roles that you could believably play. If you really feel that you need to "startle the director" into seeing a side of you that isn't easily visible, save that speech as the extra piece you've prepared just for that reason, and only if you're asked for something additional after presenting your prepared set. However, if you are asked to show two contrasting monologues (usually one from the classical and one from the contemporary repertoire), select speeches by characters you could believably play. With any audition situation, selecting age-appropriate material is expected. You should always select material that is well written, offers depth of idea and language . . . and is chosen from a play in which you could be cast. *[Have we made our feelings clear about the nature of the material you should select?]*

What is the event?
The name "monologue" is actually misleading. Although you are the only character speaking, there is nothing "mono" about the event. It is a scene, in which we only hear your side. Even a soliloquy has an intended receiver. Hamlet's famous "To be, or not to be . . ." is intended to sort out aloud an emotionally heightened turning point in the young prince's life. He is grappling with himself, and his conflicting inner self becomes the other character. In most cases, the monologue is an elongated speech in a scene between at least two people, sometimes more.

Out of the starting gate!
Many actors cheat the first beat of their monologue audition. The urge to speak is about the most important part of the entire two-minute audition speech. What has just happened? What has just been said? Who has said it? To whom? Jumping

right into your first line without first creating the context in which it is uttered is cheating you of one of the most important acting moments. That moment doesn't come at the end of the speech, or in the middle when your character suddenly breaks down and cries. The urge to speak tells us more about your character than the tears ever could.

Most monologues are not uninterrupted tirades.
The actor must leave room for nonverbal reactions by the other character(s) to what they are saying. Rapid-fire speech, no matter how heightened the emotion, may meet your audition time limit but doesn't allow you to deal with the reactions so important to any communication. The reactions of others in the scene to what you are saying (even if imagined in the audition moment) allows your character to continue—allows him or her to modify the intention throughout the speech. Take Mr. Hamlet's solo again as an example. When asking himself probing questions, isn't there a moment or two when he must actually consider what he has said? How many of us speak in paragraphs blindly without at least thinking in the moment, or without watching closely the reactions of those we're speaking to? I know of only a few people like this and I wouldn't bother having a conversation with them because it is all one-sided. That is not the point of a monologue. Sliding thoughtlessly through the language without some contemplation or awareness of how what you say is landing on others would seem almost drug-induced or manic. Acting is listening as well as speaking and this mustn't be forgotten when working solo.

Working moment-to-moment, or beat-to-beat, with the progress charted by intention and reaction is key to showing a complete moment in this character's life. Don't rush the decisions the character makes in the moment. These decisions must inform each subsequent beat throughout the monologue.

What do I do with these things at the end of my arm?

Physical life must be carefully considered. Too many auditions suffer from over-planned gestures, those that seem to come as a choice (or as blocking for all of you blockers) as opposed to a genuine kinesthetic response. "Less is more." Consider the audition room as a very small theater and the proscenium as the space that forms the fourth wall between you and the auditors. Within that space, you need to create in your mind and body the setting in which your character moves. This is why good actors possess rich imaginations. If you can imagine that you are a murderer long enough to get you through the run of Macbeth, you can imagine the setting in a non-theatrical audition space. If you can't, begin night courses in accounting and plot a career change.

How do I stop?

The final moment in your monologue is just as important as that first moment, the one that happens right before you speak. Don't cheat this moment by clipping the end of it and looking the auditors in the eye with "thank you." And by all means, only lower your head at the end of the speech if the character is directed to "fall asleep upon uttering the last syllable." It isn't a fade-to-black moment. The last impression you leave the auditors with should not be that you are a narcoleptic. Even if the speech occurs as the last moment in an act in the play, you would never lower your head as the lights fade. Don't do it here. Rather, the intention needs to be carried out, it needs to land—either in waiting for the other character's (characters') reaction or in ending the dialogue "once and for all." If you've done your work properly, the auditors will know you've finished the beat. And please, please, don't say "scene." People that employ this overtired competition tool do nothing but shatter anything that has been created before it.

After the last moment has passed, a simple "thank you" can be offered, but only if you know for certain that there won't be an interview following your presentation. "Thank you" should be reserved for your final parting comment to the auditors. It is appropriate to thank them for seeing you, but you need not thank them for watching your monologue.

What do I do when I leave the room?
Breathe. Treat yourself to a celebratory dessert, a movie, a coffee with a friend whom you really like and trust and who won't make you feel less secure. The following week, send your auditors a postcard thanking them for the time they spent with you. I've always appreciated such cards and even if they don't weigh heavily in my decision making, they remind me that the actor is a professional and considerate about his or her business. Whatever you do, don't beat yourself up after the audition even if you feel you didn't do your best. Monologue auditions are extremely difficult. Being judged on only a few awkward minutes of character creation in a decidedly un-theatrical environment is grueling and disquieting. Accept that it is a part of the ordeal of being an actor and move on with your life. If there is something about you and your work that appeals to the needs of the auditors, it will come through, even if you "blew" your big moment in the speech. You can never second-guess how the auditors feel— even the glum ones. And, after all, who wants to go to a school that doesn't want you? Who wants to be in a production that doesn't think you are right for it, or train at a school who doesn't appreciate your talent? No matter your desperation, ask yourself if you really want to be in *the* school if they don't want you? Don't forget that few actors, if any, get the role because of the school they attended.

Craig Slaight and Jack Sharrar
American Conservatory Theater
San Francisco, California

Monologues
for
Young Women

• • •

A BIRD OF PREY

Jim Grimsley

The Play: A modern tragedy set in a large city in California where the young people face good and evil on their own terms, with calamitous consequences. Centering on seventeen-year-old Monty, who has just moved with his dysfunctional family from rural Louisiana to a complex urban environment, the play explores an individual's attempt to find personal faith, while struggling to shield loved ones from the temptations and dangers they encounter every day.

Time and Place: The 1990s. An unnamed city.

The Scene: *Tracey, "a girl with a harsh view of people and the ability to express it, but very loyal to her friends," has just taunted Thacker, a "smooth, cool, charming" outsider about his friendship with the conservative, bible-carrying Monty. Hilda (fifteen to seventeen), "a girl on the fringe of popularity, slightly in love with Tracey, not yet fully conscious of it," attempts to express why she joins in with Tracey's making fun of Monty and others.*

• • •

HILDA: I don't hate him or anything. I mean, he's geeky. But there's something cute about him. I can't tell him that, because of Tracey, but I don't hate him, I don't even enjoy making fun of him, well, not all that much. I enjoy listening to Tracey when she makes fun of him because she's so good at it. I guess that's why I sit there. He's not the first person Tracey's gone after like that, but it's like he's special for her. Ever since he got here. She goes out of her way to let him know how different he is. He doesn't fit in. He is sort of cute in those ties although the tie clips are too much. He only has two. He must polish those shoes every night. Tracey says he must. She asked him if he uses spit on them, to get that shine. *(Laughs a little.)* It's not what she says, it's the way she says it. *(Pause.)* But most of the time he acts as if she isn't saying anything at all. And all you have to do is take one look at him and you know, he doesn't care whether he fits in or not. He's like a sleepwalker, I think. It's like he's not really there. *(Pause.)* I shouldn't encourage Tracey to keep after him, laughing at everything she says the way I do. But I can't help it. I care about her.

A PREFACE TO THE ALIEN GARDEN [1]
Robert Alexander

The Play: For mature audiences. *A Preface to the Alien Garden* is a contemporary "gangsta rap" that makes use of elements of *Wizard of Oz* and *Star Trek,* that centers on seventeen-year-old Lisa Body, who believes that she was abducted by aliens and returned to Earth with metal plates inserted into her. Lisa moves through her world, attempting to make sense of existence, first as an innocent, and finally as a killer.

Time and Place: The present. A black gang hideout in Kansas City.

The Scene: *Lisa "slithers, prances and struts in a butch-like manner" around G Roc, Candi, Ice Pick, and other gang members who have gathered for a meeting, making it clear that she is dedicated to violence.*

• • •

Several months have passed. It is winter.

At rise: G Roc, B Dog, Sheila, Candi, and Ice Pick are gathered at a the conference table for a meeting. They sit in a frozen pose as Lisa slithers, prances, and struts in a butch-like manner, around the frozen bodies seated at the table. She has a blue rag tied to her head and is wearing a thick, full-length, official Raiders team coat with a hood that partially obscures her blue rag.

LISA: To bang or not to bang: Is there ever any question? Gang-banging ain't no part-time thang. It's a full-time gig, you dig? I'm dedicated to the violence like it was a career. You see—bangin' is about being down for yo' homies—being down for yo' set . . . being down—when ain't nobody else down wid you. Bangin'—is getting caught and not tellin' . . . killin' and not caring and lookin' death in the face without fear.

Just because a man has the same colored flag hanging from his tail pocket—it don't mean he won't smoke yo' ass. It ain't just Crips and Bloods at each other's throats. Crips be killin' Crips like a mothafucka. Take this nigga Ice Pick for example. *(Stands behind Ice Pick.)* If he weren't in my set—I'd smoke him in a heartbeat. He's an arrogant short-sighted nigga—who thinks women ain't nothing but bitches, skeezers, and ho's. Well this is one bitch that ain't got his back.

A PREFACE TO THE ALIEN GARDEN [2]
Robert Alexander

The Play: For mature audiences. *A Preface to the Alien Garden* is a contemporary "gangsta rap" that makes use of elements of *Wizard of Oz* and *Star Trek,* that centers on seventeen-year-old Lisa Body, who believes that she was abducted by aliens and returned to Earth with metal plates inserted into her. Lisa moves through her world, attempting to make sense of existence, first as an innocent, and finally as a killer.

Time and Place: The present. A black gang hideout in Kansas City.

The Scene: *At the top of Act Two, Lisa, marking turf with her spray can, speaks of her encounter with the Aliens and the fact that she was not meant to be "earthbound."*

• • •

A month later, still winter in America.

At rise: a solitary light finds Lisa downstage right, in the Alien Garden, marking turf with her can of spray paint.

LISA: I'm a dream merchant. I've got dreams for sale—light beams for sale. This is the place to git in the space race, 'cause there're ninety-nine ways to git to Venus from here and thirty-nine ways to git to Mars. All you gotta do is click yo' heels together . . . three times to catch a light beam . . . *(A beat.)* The other day, Zeke told me the facial markings of the Ibo tribe are also worn on the faces of other Ibo warriors— many galaxies away. He told me—a time will come—when all the other Ibo warriors throughout the universe will descend upon this land, to kill all thine enemies . . . to return us to our rightful place. And those lost at birth—shall be found again.

Zeke also told me—that Monster Kody is the second coming of Malcolm X and one day he will rise from the lion's pit, he will throw off the chains that bind him, and he will lead us to the promised land, for it has already been written in the blood of the lamb. *(A beat.)*

I was not meant to be earthbound. One day I'm gonna break gravity's hold on me. I was meant to be amongst the stars. I was meant to move with the speed of light. I was meant to move like the creatures I saw—among the creatures there was something that looked like a blazing torch—constantly moving. The fire would blaze up and shoot out flashes of lightning!

(The lights become harshly bright, creating the illusion of the light from a flying saucer.)

I just stood there, as the creatures darted back and forth with the speed of lightning. As I was looking at the four creatures—I saw four wheels of light—I saw four wheels touching the ground, one beside each of the creatures. All four wheels were alike—each shone like a precious stone. The rim of the wheels were covered with eyes. Whenever the creatures moved, the wheels moved with them. And when the creatures rose up from the Earth—so did the wheels . . . every time the creatures moved or stopped or rose in the air, the wheels did exactly the same. But when I looked into the light above their heads—I saw it for the first time—a dome made of dazzling crystal—THE MOTHERSHIP—shone like a million dazzling lights.

AFTER JULIET
Sharman Macdonald

The Play: What happens after the deaths of Romeo and Juliet? What happened to Rosaline, Romeo's first love? *After Juliet*, imaginative, powerful, and poetic, resonates with a contemporary take on love and death, war and peace, as Juliet's cousin, Rosaline, who also loved Romeo, struggles to cope with the aftermath of the lovers' deaths. The Montagues and the Capulets are experiencing a tense truce while the trial of those implicated in the deaths proceeds. To complicate the situation, Benvolio, Romeo's best friend, loves Rosaline and pursues her, but she will not return his attentions because he is an enemy to her family and she seeks revenge.

Time and Place: This could be Verona. Or it could be Edinburgh, Dublin, New York, or Liverpool. It could be 1500, 1900, 2000, or 3000.

The Scene: *In a gentle rain, Rosaline (fifteen) strolls in the piazza with an umbrella and a single lily in her hand. She expresses recollections of Juliet, as Benvolio and Mercutio's surviving twin brother, Valentine, observe her.*

• • •

Rosaline walks up to a pile of flowers in the corner of the piazza. She's holding a single lily. And an umbrella.

ROSALINE: Your spirit haunts me, Juliet.
I see more of you dead
Than I did when you were alive;
(Valentine splutters with laughter.)
The drummer whirls and points.
(Benvolio puts his hand over his friend's mouth.)

That's a joke.

"More of you dead."

(She stamps her foot hard down as if knocking on the door of the grave.)

Go on laugh.

And more of you alive

Than I wanted to.

Laugh. Laugh, go on.

(Knocks again.)

Come on, Juliet.

(Benvolio pulls Valentine deep into the shadows.)

We were hardly close as cousins.

You were too small, too pretty, too rich,

Too thin and too much loved for me to cope with.

"Spoilt" is the word that springs to mind

Though I don't want to speak ill of the dead.

(She touches the stamen of the lily. Yellow nicotine pollen stains her fingers. She rubs it in.)

All a flower does is wither

It's the memories that stay for ever:

So they tell me.

So what do I recall of you?

Juliet, daddy's princess, rich,

Mummy's darling, quite a bitch.

You scratched my face once,

From here to here;

I have the scar. I have it yet.

You can see it quite clearly

In the sunlight;

A silver line.

You wanted my favorite doll.

And of course you got it.

For though I was scarred, you cried.

And your nurse swooped down

And took the moppet from me.

Spanked me hard for making you unhappy;

Gave my doll to you, her dearest baby.
Later you stole my best friend;
Wooed her with whispers;
Told her gossip's secrets;
Gave her trinkets, sweetmeats.
Later still, you took my love
And didn't know you'd done it;
Then having taken him
You let him die.
If you'd swallowed the friar's potion earlier
You would have wakened.
And my love would be alive.
None of this would have happened.
I know you, Juliet.
You hesitated, frightened.
Didn't take the stuff until the dawn.
Wakened too late in the tomb.
In the night I dream of Romeo.
He's reaching his arms out from the vault.
The poison has him in its hold.
He fills my nights with his longing for life.
Until I am afraid to go to sleep.
For though I love him still
I cannot soothe his pain.
If I could, I would
But it is not me he's reaching for.
So why, Juliet,
Should I spend my cash
On flowers for you?
Are you a saint
Simply because you were daft enough
To die for love?
Love?
A passing fancy,
No more or less.
Tomorrow or tomorrow or tomorrow

You would have tired of him.
Like your fancy for the doll;
Once possessed, you left it in the rain;
Yesterday's fancy, mud in its hair,
Damp stained the dress I'd made for her.
They think you brave to have taken your life
But you believed in immortality.
Daddy's princess could not die.
She would be there at her own funeral
To watch the tears flow
And hear her praises sung.
So you haunt me.
Don't turn away.
Listen. Listen.
What is it that you've brought about?
What trail does your fancy drag behind?
What punishments lie in your fancy's wake?
Listen, Juliet.
Come here. Come close.
Press your ear to the earth
So I know you're listening.
There's a trial going on.
Even now. In all solemnity.
Four lives hang in the balance
Forced by your selfish suicide
To take their chance
Standing at the mercy of the court.
They wait to see whether life or death
Is granted them by what we call justice.
It's a strange justice. Law meted out by the rich
Who measure their wisdom
By the weight of their gold;
As if riches bear witness to virtue.
You and I know they don't.
So four poor people are brought before the Prince
To see whether they live or die.

You brought this on them.
No feud wrought their trials.
Their misery is tribute
To your precocity.
Married. And at thirteen!
So. So. Sweet Coz.
Here. This is the last flower
You'll get from me.
Death flowers have the sweetest scent.
(She casts the flower down. Shrugs.)
That's that bit done.
(She puts down the umbrella. Stands with her face up to the rain.)

THE AUTOMATA PIETÀ [1]

Constance Congdon

The Play: In a remote part of northern Arizona, a teen fashion doll named Bambi is tossed out of a car window by her feuding "mommies"—young sisters, Jennifer and Shambhala. Abandoned in the desert, Bambi falls victim to an illegal toxic waste dumping and, mysteriously, grows to human proportions.

Time and Place: The year 2000, more or less. Northern Arizona, then New York City.

The Scene: *Vortexia, "a large young woman who speaks Spanish now and then," and a radio personality, pitches Burpee ware.*

• • •

VORTEXIA: Does anybody want some mother lovin poly-vinyl Burpee Ware? So this goes on this and you burp it. And inside is your two pieces of lettuce and your milligram of boiled chicken. Yum. I'm full.

And in this one you can put your ten white grapes. Dessert! Oh no, not another one—*please*. I couldn't possibly eat ONE MORE GRAPE!

And then, if you ever go out to dinner, and have something left over from your daily allowance of three meats, four breads, and two fruits, or is it four fruits, two meats and no breads? Because bread isn't the staff of life, you know—it's actually evil. It's made by Satan in his subterranean bakery. *Anyway*, if you have something left over when you're eating out and have put your fork down between each bite. Or, perhaps, you've been a really good girl and haven't picked up your fork in two or three years, *if* you have even a bite left over, you can put it in this purse-size Poly-vinyl Burpee Ware container and take it home to eat later—if you can take the anxiety and guilt of ever eating *again*. And then you can wash it out to use over and over, unless, of course, you've shoved it down the garbage disposal just to listen to it shred, like your pride has been shredded every time you eat or watch someone else eat while they lecture you on how to watch your weight and then give that big sigh after they've told you you have such a pretty face.

And you can use your poly-vinyl Burpee Ware containers for those homemade TV dinners of a piece of fish and green beans you can nibble at while you watch hours of soft-porn food ads and ads for diet pills and products presented by thin, thin women who are telling you what you should do about your problem when they could be drug addicts, but, hey, they still look "good."

So buy this poly-vinyl Burpee Ware with its rubber seal lid, so whatever food you haven't gulped down in that way you think all fat people eat—all that extra food will be protected for the next fat person to suck up!

THE AUTOMATA PIETÀ [2]

Constance Congdon

The Play: In a remote part of northern Arizona, a teen fashion doll named Bambi is tossed out of a car window by her feuding "mommies"—young sisters, Jennifer and Shambhala. Abandoned in the desert, Bambi falls victim to an illegal toxic waste dumping and, mysteriously, grows to human proportions.

Time and Place: The year 2000, more or less. Northern Arizona, then New York City.

The Scene: *Bambi's mommies have just tossed her out of the window of their car and landed her in a pool of toxic waste. What's happening to her? She's beginning to grow!*

• • •

BAMBI: *(Surrounded in green glow.)* What's this yucky stuff, anyway?
   (Beat.)
   Green . . . In . . . My . . . *Head.*
   (Beat.)
   Questioning the existence of God seems to be a tautological conundrum and futile, too. *What am I saying?* To question that which made me is to question the fact that I am made at all. *Help.* For, yea, I am here—before myself and have a trademark to prove it, although I have never read it myself, being unable to bend that way. Or read. Although a loquacious bobbly-toy read me the entire contents of my backside, as he spent the night under me in the corner of the closet after a rare visit from a grandmother person who cleaned all my mommies' rooms, even the big noisy yelling mommy who's angry all the time and hates her job and the

daddy. Normally, I always stay in my Party House or reside, head first, in my speed boat. Anyway, God seemed nice—I remember her plastic-wrapped hands as she assembled me and put me back on the always-forward-moving rolling floor, before I gained my outfit and accessories and—

(Really odd feeling.)

Ooooo!

'Scuse me.

(Slightly lower voice.)

ooooo! MY DRESS IS RIPPING!

OH MY!

I'M GROWING!!!!

THE AUTOMATA PIETÀ [3]
Constance Congdon

The Play: In a remote part of northern Arizona, a teen fashion doll named Bambi is tossed out of a car window by her feuding "mommies"—young sisters, Jennifer and Shambhala. Abandoned in the desert, Bambi falls victim to an illegal toxic waste dumping and, mysteriously, grows to human proportions.

Time and Place: The year 2000, more or less. Northern Arizona, then New York City.

The Scene: *Bambi, grown to human size now and still by the side of the road, contemplates the seeming futility of her present condition.*

• • •

BAMBI: Stop hopping, it doesn't help, it makes you look pathetic. It's a futile action. Futility is pathetic. Stop being pathetic. I'm sick of pathos. I'm sick of feeling sorry. The show I see by this roadside you wouldn't believe. Kittens, puppies, babies thrown out the window, WITH all the trash. Kittens and puppies can be wild, but babies don't know how. They just lay there and fuss and scream and then stare up at the big black cosmic sky, full of meaning to readers of cereal boxes and other word people, but just big, black, deaf and dumb to them. A legless spider with a zillion eyes twinkling down while they die. I've saved the ones I could and tucked them into cars stopped while their owners get rid of their internal liquids.

Perhaps you think I sound bleak. Wait until you have a Big Beach Fun House and it gets taken away. Wait until you have three perfectly good mommies and they throw you out the window. Wait.

BE AGGRESSIVE [1]

Annie Weisman

The Play: This highly imaginative, sophisticated, satirical, and poignant play depicts with affectionate understanding the adolescence of Laura, a seventeen-year-old cheerleader, whose life is abruptly changed when her mother is killed in a car crash. Suddenly forced to become caregiver to her younger sister, Hannah, and her unbending father, Phil, Laura finds escape through a fellow cheerleader, Leslie, who has found a brochure for a cheerleading camp: the Spirit Institute of the South. The two girls go against their parents' wishes and desperately follow their dream to the camp, only to make a painful discovery. The journey ultimately leads to hope and renewal, however unsettling the present may seem to be.

Time and Place: Vista Del Sol, a paradise by the sea. The present.

The Scene: *At work making "smoothies," Laura teaches some hirelings how it's done.*

• • •

Sound of a blender. Then two. Then six. Then all the blenders of the southland, whirring at top speed. Lights up on the smoothie shop. Laura with her hand on the top of a blender. Her body shakes. Then stops.

LAURA: 'K. First you add the Basic Boost.

(Adds something to the blender. Puts on the top. Loud blending sound again. Her body shakes. It stops.) Now the All-Pro Protein. *(Adds something.)* Then, ask if they've tried any of our Smoothie madditives, which are: Mood Lift, Memory Boost, Energina, Youth Jolt, and Mega-Cleanse. Then, tell

them about this week's promotional madditive, which is— *(Checks list.)* Moby Thick!—a fiber blend made from the baleen of humpback whales whose healthful benefits have been enjoyed by the Inuit people for centuries. And we guarantee these whales died naturally by old age and not poaching or disease. *(Beat.)* Then, they pick their fruit. Oh, you're supposed to try to push the new fruits. Otherwise, people will just get like, strawberry or banana. There's a new hybrid of kiwi and cassava melon—it's called Kissava—and it has twice the mineral content of an average serving of fruit. You're supposed to say that. *(Beat.)* Oh, and the cool thing is, no matter what you put in, you always add our special smoothie starter at the end. That way, the color always comes out the same. The healthful rosy flush that customers want. If you forget this final additive, the color will be grayish brown. And when they see, they won't like it. *(Beat.)* Oh, and if you mess it up, just throw it away and do it over. We never run out of anything. Somebody comes in at night and stocks it all, I guess. *(Pause.)* I don't know how. Some of the stuff is like, really heavy. *(Beat.)* 'K, that's it. That's all you need to know. *(Pause.)* Now blend! *(Noise of a thousand blenders. Lights shift.)*

BE AGGRESSIVE [2]

Annie Weisman

The Play: This highly imaginative, sophisticated, satirical, and poignant play depicts with affectionate understanding the adolescence of Laura, a seventeen-year-old cheerleader, whose life is abruptly changed when her mother is killed in a car crash. Suddenly forced to become caregiver to her younger sister, Hannah, and her unbending father, Phil, Laura finds escape through a fellow cheerleader, Leslie, who has found a brochure for a cheerleading camp: the Spirit Institute of the South. The two girls go against their parents' wishes and desperately follow their dream to the camp, only to make a painful discovery. The journey ultimately leads to hope and renewal, however unsettling the present may seem to be.

Time and Place: Vista Del Sol, a paradise by the sea. The present.

The Scene: *Laura remembers her mother and contemplates the transitory circumstances of our daily life.*

• • •

LAURA: In 1971, my mom was alive, and she's dead now. In 1971, my mother was alive, and today, she's gone.
[LESLIE: But she's always in your heart.]
LAURA: *(Beat.)* She used to tell us things, but I barely remember and I can't ask her again! I can't say hey, Mom, tell me things I never listened to! Tell me how to do things! Tell me how to bake sugar cookies so they're soft in the middle! Tell me how to sweep my hair up so it holds with just a pin! Tell me what it feels like when your water breaks and a baby comes out! I don't have anybody to tell me that! *(Beat.)* In 1971, she had a gray streak in the front of her hair. Premature

gray. She had it for years until she finally got sick of the giggles and stares and she dyed it like the rest of them. I don't even remember barely. I was so little. *(Beat.)* Is that what happens? You're young, and you believe in things, and then you what? You get married, you have kids, you move into a Spanish stucco ocean-view unit and you forget? One day you wear your white streak like a peacock's tail, and the next day you're letting them paint it with bleach and toner and wrap it in tin foil and you're sitting under a hair dryer to cook for an hour while you learn lightening tips from a beauty magazine! Like everybody else! *(Beat.)* When you sit under those dryer domes, you can't see or hear a thing. You just have to sit there quietly and let all that stuff soak into you. *(Beat.)* She's really kind of been gone for a long long time. *(Pause.)* I don't want to be a dead girl. I want to be a person who's alive. *(She turns and starts to slowly walk away.)*

BREATH, BOOM [1]

Kia Corthron

The Play: Kia Corthron's *Breath, Boom* depicts the violent world of streetwise teenage gangsters in the Bronx, N.Y.— particularly a bunch of feuding "sisters." A world in which it's the norm to never have known your father, to have been raped at five by your mother's boyfriend, and to then have your mother murder the boyfriend and be thrown in jail. Such is the world of Prix, the play's central character, a tough, ruthless sixteen-year-old whose life is measured by detention, counseling, drug running, and jail—a life where the only escape is in her fascination with fireworks: glorious, showering, chaotic lights of color in the darkness.

Time and Place: The present. Bronx, N.Y.

The Scene: *In jail, Prix shares time with Cat, another young inmate. Cat ruminates on their condition behind bars.*

• • •

(During Cat's next speech, Jerome enters the cell, eyes on Prix. Prix sees him; Cat doesn't. He exits. Prix goes back to her sketching.)

CAT: I hear 'em! Cryin' on the phone, "My honey, my honey," "I miss my friend." Most of 'em's honeys was kickin' the shit out of 'em daily and their *friends?* Their best girlfriend's on the outside and so's their honey guess what one plus one is equalin'? *(Beat.)* Could be worse. See them ugly green one-piece things they make the women wear? Least adolescents, we wear our own shit. *(Beat.)* Easy time. Five months you be eighteen, outta here, eleven left for me, shit. Scotfree both us and I'm fifteen, three more years a minor, I get caught, easy time. Eleven months I *know* my roof? I *know* my mealtimes? shit. Damn sure beats the fosters.

[PRIX: *Usually all I hear's you whinin' 'bout the clothes situation.*]

CAT: Lacka choices! I *love* my clothes, but wearin' the same five outfits gets limitin' after awhile. There's this cute thing I useta wear, black, kinda sheer, kinda spare, my belly button on the open-air market. They say No way, Stupid! Their Nazi dress code, what. They think wearin' it'll get me pregnant? in *here? (Beat.)* Ain't my first time in. Fourth!

[PRIX: *Runaway.*]

CAT: Three more years I'm a fuckin' criminal for it! can't wait 'til eighteen! Runnin' away I be legal! *(Beat.)* My broken arm was mindin' its own business wisht they'da minded theirs, dontcha never believe that crap about best to tell the counselor tell the teacher it'll make things better. Cuz ya *will* get sent back home and just when ya thought things could get no worse, they do.

[PRIX: *Sh!*]

(Prix moves toward the wall, leans against it. Someone is tapping against it, a code. Prix taps back in code. When the communication is complete, Prix sits back down to her sketching. Cat smiles.)

CAT: What's the big one? Single most thing earned you all the gracious undivided esteem? I heard this: shot a enemy girl in the face. Then went to her funeral cuz yaw was best friends second grade, made all your sisters go, put the whole goddamn family on edge and every one of 'em knew and not a one of 'em said a word about it to you. *(Beat.) And* one time jumpin' a girl in, she not too conscious, you jump your whole weight on her face ten times maybe? twelve? 'fore a sister pull you off. *And* when yaw stand around, eenie meenie minie pick some herb comin' down the subway steps to steal their wallet, you was the one everybody know could always knock 'em out first punch. *And* one time on a revenge spree, dress up like a man so no one identify you later, stick your hair under a cap and shoot dead some boy ten years old. *And—*

> [PRIX: *Fifteen. (Pause. Cat is confused.) I don't kill no kids. Fifteen.*]

CAT: O.G.! you gonna earn it. Original Gangsta, people respect you long after you retire Take me in! *(No answer.)* You get it. The high, right? This girl Aleea, she tell me all about it. The kickin' and smashin' and breakin' bones snap! Somebody lyin' in a flood a their own blood, somebody dead it gets her all hyped up, thrill thing! And power, them dead you not, *you* made it happen! Them dead, *you* done it! You ever get that high?

BREATH, BOOM [2]
Kia Corthron

The Play: Kia Corthron's *Breath, Boom* depicts the violent world of streetwise teenage gangsters in the Bronx, N.Y.—particularly a bunch of feuding "sisters." A world in which it's the norm to never have known your father, to have been raped at five by your mother's boyfriend, and to then have your mother murder the boyfriend and be thrown in jail. Such is the world of Prix, the play's central character, a tough, ruthless sixteen-year-old whose life is measured by detention, counseling, drug running, and jail—a life where the only escape is in her fascination with fireworks: glorious, showering, chaotic lights of color in the darkness.

Time and Place: The present. Bronx, N.Y.

The Scene: *Cat expresses admiration for Prix's cold, ruthless power.*

• • •

Cell. As Cat chatters she pulls the sheet off the upper bunk, then sits tying it. She is cheery. Prix reads a tattered paperback black romance novel, she does not look at Cat.

CAT: *(Admiration:)* You the coldest fish I know! Ruthless! People know it too, you walk into a room, silence! *(New idea:)* Prix. Come to my geometry tomorrow. I like geometry but those dumb bitches just come in bitchin', bitchin' interrupt the class then I don't learn nothin' but you walk in, everybody shut up, everybody know who you are get quiet fast, come on, geometry! I like that math. Circles is three-sixty, a line goes on and on, rectangle versus the parallelogram, interestin'! Ain't fireworks geometry? Can't the study a angles and arcs be nothin' but helpful? Come on! Favor for me?

(Prix chuckles to herself. Cat doesn't necessarily expect the refusal, but is delighted by it.)

CAT: I know! You don't do favors! You the coldest fish I know! *(Beat.)* You met Ms. Bramer? She's the new current events she's nice I hope she stick around awhile. She say the 6 o'clock news always hypin': "Tough on teens! Youth violence outa hand, try 'em like adults!" But she say news never say three times as many murders committed by late forties as by under-eighteens, Ms. Bramer say news never mention for every one violence committed by an under-eighteens, *three* violence committed by adults *to* under-eighteens. Ms. Bramer say if we violent where we learn it? Sow what you reap.

[PRIX: Reap what you sow.]

CAT: *(Having just noticed Prix's reading material:)* I know that book! passed to me months ago. She's a lawyer, pro bono, he's a big record producer. He's rich and she appreciates it but she don't know, loooves him but got that lawyer's degree and don't know she can lower herself to *that.* I didn't think you read that stuff, I love you and roses and wet eyes. *(Beat.)* You ever plan your funeral?

[PRIX: Fireworks.]

CAT: Nothin' somber for me, I got the tunes all picked out, went through my CD collection I know who my special guest stars be, I figure they come, like this poor unfortunate fifteen-year-old girl died, ain't the city violent and sad? We felt so depressed we come give a free funeral concert, her last request. Good publicity for them. Here's the processional tune: *(Begins humming a lively hip-hop piece, interrupts herself.)* processional, when the people first walks in with the casket. *(Resumes her humming, stops.)* My coffin's gonna be open. Yours? *(Prix turns a page.)* I'm gonna look good, I got the dress picked and I want people to see it. You ever plan your suicide?

[PRIX: Fifth grade.]

CAT: Pills? Gun stuck up your mouth?

> *[PRIX: Off the Brooklyn Bridge. (Now puzzled.) Would that kill ya?]*

CAT: World Trade Center better bet, know how many free-fall floors to concrete? Hundred ten!

BREATH, BOOM [3]

Kia Corthron

The Play: Kia Corthron's *Breath, Boom* depicts the violent world of streetwise teenage gangsters in the Bronx, N.Y.— particularly a bunch of feuding "sisters." A world in which it's the norm to never have known your father, to have been raped at five by your mother's boyfriend, and to then have your mother murder the boyfriend and be thrown in jail. Such is the world of Prix, the play's central character, a tough, ruthless sixteen-year-old whose life is measured by detention, counseling, drug running, and jail—a life where the only escape is in her fascination with fireworks: glorious, showering, chaotic lights of color in the darkness.

Time and Place: The present. Bronx, N.Y.

The Scene: *Prix speaks of her dream to design fireworks.*

• • •

[COMET: Whatchu wanna do? Shoot 'em off?]
PRIX: Design 'em. *(Works quietly, then.) And* shoot 'em off. Fireworks people ain't a architect, make the blueprint and give to someone else to build. Clothes designer never touch a sewin' machine. A fireworks artist, take your basic chrysanthemum, not to be confused with peonies, the latter comprised a dots but chrysanthemums with petal tails, the big flower, start with a pistil of orange then move out into blue, blue which comes from copper or chlorine, cool blue burstin' out from orange pistil, blue instantly change to strontium nitrate red to sodium yellow, cool to warm, warmer and the designer ain't the joyful bystander, she's right there pushin' the buttons and while the crowd's oohin' aahin' this'n she's already on to the next button. This quick chrysanthemum I'd start my show with and accompanying reports of course,

bang bang and I'll throw in a few willows, slower timin' and a softer feelin', tension to relaxation keep the audience excited, anticipatin', then time for multiple-breakers, shell breakin' into a flower breakin' 'to another flower 'to another, then a few comets *(Points to drawing on the wall; refers to Comet.)* Comets! Then, *then* if I had a bridge, a *Niagara*, fallin' from the edge and this wouldn't even be the finale, maybe . . . maybe . . . somethin' gooey, like "Happy Birthday Comet!" *Now* finale, which of course is the bombs and the bombs and the bombs and "chaos" can't possibly be the description cuz this be the most precisely planned chaos you ever saw! *Hanabi!* flowers of fire. My show people screamin' it, "*Hanabi! Hanabi!*"

BROKEN HALLELUJAH

Sharman Macdonald

The Play: During the longest siege of a city in American history, *Broken Hallelujah* is set in the smoky hollows of war-
torn Petersburg, Virginia, where two girls have a life-altering
encounter with one Confederate and two Union soldiers.
Scottish playwright Macdonald explores the effects of the
failing American Civil War on young soldiers and citizens in
this new play, co-commissioned by A.C.T.'s Young
Conservatory New Plays Program and Theatre Royal Bath.
Rich in language and boldly truthful, *Broken Hallelujah* is a
story of the effects of war on young people that is as timely
as today's newspaper headlines. The young characters in this
remarkable play have had little input in what ultimately will
be their fate. Pawns in a decidedly adult conflict, the youth
engaged in the siege of Petersburg must consider a future
over which they have little control.

Time and Place: June, 1864, to April, 1865. Petersburg,
Virginia

The Scene: *Young Maureen ponders the increasing devasta-
tion the war is exacting on the human condition.*

• • •

MAUREEN: There are towns south of here. In Tennessee there
are towns. In Alabama there are towns and the towns are
empty of men. They're just empty of men. All the men from
the towns are dead. And the ladies have no husbands. And
the children have no fathers. And the girls have no sweet-
hearts. I hear the war will go on and on til all the towns are
like that. Til there's only women left in all the towns of the
Confederacy. Only then will the war end . . . The big guns just
tear men apart and spread their vitals over the earth til

there's lakes of blood and bridges to walk on over the lakes of blood and these bridges they are made of flesh. The biggest enemy of a soldier is his bowels, and his feet, and his lungs. You hear their lungs. In the morning when their drums roll to wake them up you hear the whole army cough. Thousands of men coughing all at once—coughing so hard you can't hear the drums anymore. Can you tell a Confederate cough from a Yankee cough? I can't. That's the strangest thing. We think different, we talk different, we smell different. Wouldn't you think we'd cough different? Measles have killed more men than ever the guns have. More men have died of dysentery, and scarlet fever and mumps and the typhus than ever died of bullet wounds. I'm half the girl I was now September's come. I'm half the girl I was on the fifteenth of June when these people started besieging us, my mother says. I'll be half again by the time they go. Then no man will ever want me. A man wants flesh on the bones he holds in his arms. Man sees me half the weight I am now he'll think I've got the galloping consumption and he'll never marry me.

BURIED CHILD

Sam Shepard

The Play: Amidst the squalor of a decaying farm, a family harbors a deep-seated unhappiness that has led to destructive suppressed anger and violence—all born of a long-hidden secret. The drunken, ranting Dodge and Halie, his alcoholic wife, fight their way through each grim day, accompanied by their misbegotten sons, Tilden, a hulking ex-All-American football player, and Bradley, who has lost a leg in a chainsaw accident. When Vince, a grandson none of them recollects, enters their world with his girlfriend, Shelly, Tilden is compelled to unearth the family secret, and the possibility of redemption finally seems plausible.

Time and Place: A farmhouse.

The Scene: *Shelly, overcome by the madness that surrounds her, lashes out at Halie and Dewis, a local Protestant minister of dubious distinction.*

• • •

SHELLY: Don't come near me! Don't anyone come near me. I don't need any words from you, I'm not threatening anybody. I don't even know what I'm doing here. You all say you don't remember Vince, OK, maybe you don't. Maybe it's Vince that's crazy. Maybe he's made this whole family thing up. I don't even care anymore. I was just coming along for the ride. I thought it'd be a nice gesture. Besides, I was curious. He made all of you sound familiar to me. Every one of you. For every name, I had an image. Every time he'd tell me a name, I'd see the person. In fact, each of you was so clear in my mind that I actually believed it was you. I really believed when I walked through that door that the people who lived here would turn out to be the same people in my imagination. But

I don't recognize any of you. Not one. Not even the slightest resemblance.

CHANGES OF HEART [1]

Pierre Carlet de Chamblain de Marivaux

Translated and adapted by Stephen Wadsworth

The Play: Stephen Wadsworth's fine and playable translation and adaptation of eighteenth-century French playwright Marivaux's *Changes of Heart*, explores the deep question: What happens within the human spirit when one dares to love the person one could not imagine loving? True to Marivaux's original, the play makes use of word play and traditional characters drawn from Italian commedia: Harlequin, Flaminia, Silvia, and Trivelin. When a Prince kidnaps Harlequin's love, Silvia, and takes her to his court, Harlequin pursues her, only to become embroiled in a complex set of circumstances that lead to a remarkable outcome.

Time and Place: About 1750, France. Court of a Prince.

The Scene: *Silvia, in a rage because she has been separated from her true love, Harlequin, takes out her frustrations on her servant, Trivelin.*

• • •

SYLVIA: Very well, *my servant,* you think so highly of the honor shown me here—what do I need idle ladies-in-waiting spying on me for? They take away my lover and replace him with *women?* Hardly adequate compensation! And what do I care about all the singing and dancing they force me to sit through? A village girl happy in a little town is worth more than a princess weeping in a gorgeous suite of rooms. If the prince is so young and beautiful and full of desire, it's not my fault. He should keep all that for his equals and leave me to my poor Harlequin, who is no more a man of means than I am a woman of leisure, who is not richer than I am or fancier than I am, and who doesn't live in a bigger house than I do, but who *loves* me, without guile or pretense, and whom I love in return in the same way, and for whom I will die of a broken heart if I don't see him again soon. And what have they done to *him?* Perhaps they are mistreating him . . . *(Silvia's rage peaks.)* I am so angry! This is so unfair! You are my servant? Get out of my sight, I cannot abide you!

CHANGES OF HEART [2]

Pierre Carlet de Chamblain de Marivaux

Translated and adapted by Stephen Wadsworth

The Play: Stephen Wadsworth's fine and playable translation and adaptation of eighteenth-century French playwright Marivaux's *Changes of Heart*, explores the deep question: What happens within the human spirit when one dares to love the person one could not imagine loving? True to Marivaux's original, the play makes use of word play and traditional characters drawn from Italian commedia: Harlequin, Flaminia, Silvia, and Trivelin. When a Prince kidnaps Harlequin's love, Silvia, and takes her to his court, Harlequin pursues her, only to become embroiled in a complex set of circumstances that lead to a remarkable outcome.

Time and Place: About 1750, France. Court of a Prince.

The Scene: *Still upset at her separation from Harlequin, Silvia bemoans to Flaminia the "dreadful" court life and people who surround her.*

• • •

Flaminia and Silvia are in the middle of a conversation.

SILVIA: You're the only person around here I can tolerate, and you seem to have my interests at heart, I don't trust the rest of them. [Where is Harlequin?]
　[*FLAMINIA: He's still eating.*]
SILVIA: You know, this place is really dreadful. I've never seen people so . . . *polite*. There are *so* many curtseys, *so* many pretty speeches—you'd think they were the best people in the world, that they're full of integrity and good intentions. But no, not at all. There's not one of them who hasn't come

to me and said oh-so-discreetly, "Mademoiselle, believe me, you're better off forgetting Harlequin and marrying the Prince." And they say this to me absolutely without a qualm, as if they were encouraging me to do the right thing! "But," I say to them, "I gave my promise to Harlequin. What about fidelity, honor, good faith?" They don't even know what I'm talking about. They laugh in my face and tell me I'm being childish, that a proper young lady ought to be reasonable, isn't *that* nice! To hold nothing sacred, to cheat one's fellow man, to go back on one's word, to be two-faced and to lie— *that's* how to be a proper young lady? Who *are* these people? Where do they come from? What dough did they make them out of?

THE CONFESSIONS OF MAX TIVOLI (FICTION)

Andrew Sean Greer

The Play: This fascinating story offers an original exploration and perspective on questions of age, friendship, and love. Max Tivoli is born in the appearance of a miniature old man, but as he grows up and becomes wiser, his body becomes younger and younger. At seventeen, when he appears fifty-three years of age, he falls in love with Alice, the girl next door. Before their love can be realized, though, Max must appear younger and Alice grow older. Only Max's parents, Alice, and his best friend, Hughie, know the secret of his aging. Late in life, Max makes a painful discovery: his best friend is the real love of Alice's life.

Time and Place: 1898, San Francisco, California.

The Scene: *Alice (sixteen) sits in the backyard garden of her house, where Max, now seventeen but appearing in his mid-fifties, has been keeping her company. Alice expresses her wish that she had lived in another time.*

• • •

ALICE: I think maybe I was born in the wrong time . . . Tonight, for instance. I love it tonight. Nothing modern. No kerosene lamps smelling things up, or gaslight. Hurts your eyes. No groups of people crowded around a stereoscope, or a piano singing another round of "Grandfather Clock" for heck's sake. I wish every night was just starlight and candles and nothing to do. We would have so much time.

It's hard to image such a different life. We'd think about light all the time. You know that when it got dark in winter and there wasn't much light, you would have to do everything before sundown, well, there weren't any streetlights on country roads back then, were there? How frightening. And you couldn't read at night except by candlelight, and you probably saved your candles very carefully. Not like us. You made your own, they were everything to you, if you read books. And you had to read, what else was there to do? They had so few nice clothes they never went out. They didn't have parlors or nonsense like Wardian cases and kaleidoscopes or watching magic lantern shows. There wasn't any of that to do. There were just . . . people. Think of it.

I mean a long time ago. I mean before kerosene lamps, and I don't mean special evenings like balls, I mean evenings like this. Ones we like to kill with parlor games. How could anyone fall in love by gaslight, I ask you?

CRUMBS FROM THE TABLE OF JOY
Lynn Nottage

The Play: A complex, thought-provoking play, *Crumbs from the Table of Joy* tells the story of an African-American family recently relocated from Florida to Brooklyn in search of a better life: the recently widowed Godfrey and his daughters, Ernestine (Ernie) and Ermina. Once arrived, their lives move through a series of unsettling incidents as the girls' politically and socially active aunt, Lily, makes her presence felt. Godfrey, who has turned to religion, eventually finds a new wife in Gerte, a quiet German immigrant who suffered through the horrors of World War II. Godfrey attempts to keep the family together, but the girls, particularly Ernie, is closer to her spiritual mother, Lily, and sets off for Harlem to find her and a new life.

Time and Place: 1950s. Brooklyn, N.Y.

The Scene: *Ernestina, having escaped to the movies for awhile, finds herself on a crowded street corner in Harlem looking for her aunt, Lily Ann Green.*

• • •

ERNESTINE: *(To audience.)* In the movies the darkness precedes everything. In the darkness, the theater whispers with anticipation . . . *(Ernestine stands, she's on a crowded street corner in Harlem. Lost and confused on the noisy street corner.)* Finally, Harlem . . . Lost, "does anybody know how I get to Lenox Avenue? Lenox Avenue? The Party headquarters! You know, Lily Ann Green. Lily Ann Green. Lily . . ." *(Ernestine holds out a sheet of paper.)* Nothing's there but an empty bar "Chester's." Blue flashing neon, sorta nice. I order a sloe gin fizz and chat with the bartender about the weather. It looks like rain. It's only men. They make me nervous. But they remember Lily. Everyone does. So I tell them, "I've come to enlist, in the revolution of course. To fight, the good fight. I got a high school diploma. I'll do anything. I'll scrub floors if need be. You see, I care very much about the status of the Negro in this country. We can't just sit idly by, right? Lily said we used to live communally in Africa and solve our differences through music by creating riffs off of a simple timeline building out toward something extraordinary, like . . . bebop." The bartender tells me he knows just the place I'm looking for, address 137th Street between Convent and Amsterdam. And here I find myself standing before this great Gothic city rising out of Harlem. Black, gray stone awash. At the corner store they tell me it's . . . City College. *(A moment.)* In the movies . . . well. . . . Years from now I'll ride the subway back to Brooklyn. I'll visit Daddy and Gerte and we'll eat a huge meal of bratwurst and sweet potatoes and realize that we all escape somewhere and take comfort sometimes in things we don't understand. And before I graduate Ermina will give birth to her first child, lovely Sandra. She'll move home with Nana for a few years and she'll be the one to identify Lily's cold body poked full of holes her misery finally borne out. Years from now I'll read the *Communist Manifesto, The Souls of Black Folks,* and *Black Skin, White Masks* and find my dear Lily amongst the pages. Still years from now I'll remember my mother and the sweet-smelling humid afternoons by the Florida waters, and then years from now I'll ride the Freedom bus back down home enraged and vigilant, years from now I'll marry a civil servant and argue about the Vietnam war, integration, and the Black Panther movement. Years from now I'll send off one son to college in New England and I'll lose the other to drugs and sing loudly in the church choir. *(She lifts her suitcase, beaming.)* But today I'm just riffing and walking as far as these feet will take me. Walking . . . riffing . . . riffing . . . riffing. *(Lights slowly fade as Ernestine continues to repeat the line over and over again. A song like "Some Enchanted Evening" gives way to a bebop version of the song. Blackout.)*

DUST [1]

Sarah Daniels

The Play: In this imaginative, time-warping tale, a group of students traveling through London become stranded on a train in the Underground. When one of the girls, Flavia (fifteen), leaves the group to find a way out on her own, she mysteriously enters a new dimension and is transformed into a girl gladiator in ancient Roman London. Here she encounters the great and mythic heroine, Boudicca.

Time and Place: The present. London, Underground.

The Scene: *Boudicca, the warrior queen, has just made her appearance to Flavia the scene before, and now speaks to the audience of what it's been like on the "other" side.*

• • •

BO: *(To the audience.)* If she thinks it's lonely there, it's much worse here. Are you listening? I said it's much worse here. Oh I know I've got some great company. Virginia Woolf, Sylvia Plath, Marilyn M, Del Shannon, Kurt Cobain. Music? If music be the food of love, no wonder I'm on my own. The racket I've had to get used to. I don't like to judge but some of the stuff those people call tunes sounds worse than when Caligula's horse got its head trapped under the wheel of a chariot. Lovely people though, most of them. The artists anyway. Got a couple of weirdos. One with a small moustache who quite frankly was lucky to have got off so lightly, dying by his own hand. I put him in a room of his own straight away. You can imagine how Virginia kicked off about that. Then there's a lovely monk who set himself a light. I've got a few of those actually. I said right out to their faces. I said "nice action but wrong target," babes. How we all ended up may have taken more courage than most could muster in a lifetime, but whichever way you look at it we still finished it off with an act of cowardice. Oh yes. Taken me centuries to come to terms with that. Me! Me, who rode around fearlessly reeking revenge, wrecking their cosy life styles. But when they turned and came looking for me, I could see the way it was going. And I knew, this was it. My chickens were coming home to roast. So I said to myself, "OK Big Bo, time to go." I took such last-resort pleasure in picturing their disappointment when they found I'd got myself rather than let them get me. But hey, they got over it. It took them all of a morning, and then they got on with their conquering and forgot all about me. When life doesn't go on, when it stops—then that is it. It really is. The end of all possibilities. I should know. If could have my life again the one thing I'd do is not kill myself. And it's not just me. We all think that here.

DUST [2]
Sarah Daniels

The Play: In this imaginative, time-warping tale, a group of students traveling through London become stranded on a train in the Underground. When one of the girls, Flavia (fifteen), leaves the group to find a way out on her own, she mysteriously enters a new dimension and is transformed into a girl gladiator in ancient Roman London. Here a poverty-stricken woman encounters Boudicca, the mythic heroine who led a revolt against the Roman occupation of Britain.

Time and Place: The present. London, Underground.

The Scene: *Woman with a baby, a poverty-stricken beggar, appears in both past and present as representative of those who share her plight through all of history.*

• • •

WOMAN WITH A BABY: *(Although she obviously no longer has the baby.) (Directly to the audience:)* I was the girl whose panties stank of poverty, who grew up to be a woman who smelt of stale breast milk, who gave birth then turned her face to the wall, who gave her baby away, whose kid died for lack of food, out of neglect, who used her dead baby to smuggle drugs, who abandoned her child on the train to Auschwitz, who murdered her offspring in a fit of jealous rage at its innocent lack of anxiety.

You look at me like I'm the shit on your shoes but you can not shake my dust from your feet. You've drawn me into your lungs but you want to suffocate me cos I'm now part of you. I have always been with you.

You have always reveled in reviling me but you have no room to breathe because after two thousand years of your civilization I am still alive and thriving amongst you and you are more concerned with making sure animals don't become extinct than with trying to eradicate me.

DUST [3]

Sarah Daniels

The Play: In this imaginative, time-warping tale, a group of students traveling through London become stranded on a train in the Underground. When one of the girls, Flavia (fifteen), leaves the group to find a way out on her own, she mysteriously enters a new dimension and is transformed into a girl gladiator in ancient Roman London.

Time and Place: The present. London, Underground.

The Scene: *Trifosa, a Roman "Girlie" gladiator, has now reached the "other" side, having been torn to bits by a lion in the stadium.*

• • •

TRIFOSA: *(Doing or fiddling with her nails.)* I didn't quite know what to expect when I reached the other side. Well of course, I wasn't expecting to reach the other side so suddenly. And I wasn't expecting it to be like this. Trifosa is a pet name given to me by my parents. It means delicious. Well, the big cat back there certainly thought so. I know you've got my number. I always thought of myself as special, better than the rest. The fat, the hopeless, and the weedy kid right from the time we all had to play in the sandpit together always got on my nerves. I couldn't stand their humorless, lifeless miserable whining. I got pleasure baiting them. The more I did it the more I wanted to and the better I became at it. And I could barely conceal my smile when, because of me, they cried. Sometimes, even on my own I would laugh out loud the memory was so pleasurable. I never touched them, much less hit or assaulted them but here I've been given a worse room than a whole heap of mass murderers. What's more they're allowed to sleep whereas I haven't been allowed so much as a catnap. Someone out the back just told me that I'll probably have to start again and for every horrible thing I said or did back then, I'll have to do a good one. How long will that take? It makes me exhausted just thinking about it.

FINER NOBLE GASES

Adam Rapp

The Play: Described as an "existential rock & roll comedy," *Finer Noble Gases* portrays the flattened dreams and fatal visions of four aimless East-Village musicians (Staples, Speed, Chase, and Lynch) whose existence has fallen into purposeless TV watching and drug addiction. Into their life sometimes appears Dot, a little girl from downstairs, who adds further pathos to a decimated environment.

Time and Place: An East Village apartment near Tomkins Square Park in New York. Winter.

The Scene: *Dot (eleven) is watching TV with two of the musicians, who are mesmerized by the death of an animal on one of those "nature" programs. She reflects on one of her favorite past times at school.*

• • •

DOT: In the library at my junior high they have these huge computer monitors. The size of small refrigerators. Three-feet high some of them. The most beautiful screen savers you'll ever see. Mountains. Waterfalls. Pictures of magic cities. Colors that haven't even been invented yet. If you stand next to the hard drives and listen real close you can hear them singing. Like hummingbirds. A gazillion megahertz of ram just whirling away. *(Standing, gliding slowly toward the TV.)* Sometimes I go real early in the morning. When nobody's there. And I just listen. I listen for a while and then for some reason I hug each monitor. One by one. There's like fifty of them. *(Hugging Gray's TV now.)* I hug each one and I get a little part of that song inside me. It's the most beautiful way to start the day. *(Breaking from the hug.)* I think those birds on the rhinos are so cool.

[*STAPLES: It's like someone put 'em there.*]
(*Dot glides to the ottoman, sits.*)

DOT: In the library there's this one African Grassland screen saver with little birds. They ride around on this elephant and eat the bugs off its back. There's a lion, too, but he doesn't do anything. The elephant walks around and drinks water out of the wallows. That's where the rhinos play with their kids.

THE LESS THAN HUMAN CLUB

Timothy Mason

The Play: Davis Daniels, a troubled young man, recreates a turbulent year in his life (1968) with the hopes of finding answers to paths that have led to today. The journey back replays the complexities of relationships, the crisis of sexual identity, the bonds of truthful friendship, and the search for purpose.

Time and Place: Fall 1967; winter/spring of 1968. Minneapolis, Minnesota.

The Scene: *Kirsten, a shy high school junior, whom Davis has invited to the "Snow Daze" dance, nervously makes conversation—it's her first date. In reality she is just a cover for Davis, who is struggling with his sexual identity.*

• • •

KIRSTEN: You're a wonderful dancer. I mean, you never go to dances, where did you learn to dance like that? You're just amazing. *(Beat.)* My dad helps me with so much, he's such a great guy, I mean, he's a little quiet, he's a mailman. They tend to be quiet, letter carriers, they think a lot. I don't think people generally realize that. *(Beat.)* Walk and think, think and walk. *(Looks at her melting Dixie cup of hot cider.)* Oh, no! I just knew it! I knew Dixie cups were a mistake! Miss Borders said she didn't think it would be a problem and I said, "Oh yes it will, you just wait!" That woman just doesn't listen. Sorry, I shouldn't criticize. It's like Thumper's dad was always saying to him, "If you can't say somethin' nice, don't say nothin' at all." In *Bambi*. The movie? It was my favorite movie when I was a kid. Remember it? If you want to go Davis, I'll understand. I know you're thinking this was a mistake. You're a kind person, you always have been. But I'll understand.

(Beat.) My dad was so nervous tonight, you'd think he was the one going on a . . . to a dance. And a little proud, too, I think, you know? But mostly just nervous. He felt better when he met you, I could tell. Did he give you the old third degree while I was upstairs? I think my dad's a lot more like Thumper's dad than Bambi's dad. Of course Bambi's dad was a great big stag and the King of the Forest and my dad's a lot more like an old rabbit. Bambi's mom died around the same time mine did. I mean, that's about when I saw that movie, right around the time my mom died, and we both missed our moms terribly. I think of all the things I should have said to her but didn't. I guess that's why you mourn. Then you go on. Like Bambi did. *(Beat.)* This is the first time I ever went out with a boy. I think my dad was afraid I was going to get all twitter-pated tonight and that's why he was so nervous. At Luther League at church they pair you off for parties or hayrides but that's different. A boy tried to kiss me once on a hayride but I didn't like him so I didn't let him. There was a boy at church I sort of liked but he moved. *(Beat.)* Let me take these, they're undrinkable.

THE MISS FIRECRACKER CONTEST

Beth Henley

THE MISS FIRECRACKER CONTEST

By Beth Henley

The Play: The tale of Carnelle Scott, a young woman with bright red hair, who dreams of escaping her humdrum existence in rural Mississippi. She enters "The Miss Firecracker Contest," the local 4th of July beauty pageant, and puts her tap-dancing and baton-twirling talents to use in a "Star Spangles Banner" routine. With a few sparklers tossed in, she's sure to take the title and find her way out of town in a trail of glory, unless falling in love along the way with a fellow who was recently released from a mental institution gets in the way.

Time and Place: Late June and early July. Brookhaven, Mississippi, small Southern town.

The Scene: Carnelle confides her hopes and dreams to Popeye Jackson, her new friend and the seamstress of her patriotic ensemble of red, blue, and silver. Note: The dialogue in brackets can be eliminated to allow a solo speech.

• • •

CARNELLE: Well it's just like my aunt Rondelle fixed it up. It's got her special touch. This old spinning wheel; these lace doilies; these old pictures in frames here. I'd prefer something more modern and luxurious, but—that's just me.
    [POPEYE: You live here with your aunt?]
CARNELLE: *[Oh, no.]* She died. She had cancer.
    [POPEYE: I'm sorry.]

CARNELLE: It happened just a few weeks before last Christmas. We were very close. It was a tragedy.

[POPEYE: *I'm sorry.*]

CARNELLE: (*As she pours Popeye's tea.*) You may of heard about her; Ronelle Williams? It was a famous medical case—ran in all the newspapers.

[POPEYE: *No.*]

[CARNELLE: *Well, see what it was—Do you take lemon?*]

[POPEYE: *Please.*]

CARNELLE: Anyway, she had this cancer of the pituitary gland, I believe it was; so what they did was they replaced her gland with the gland of a monkey to see if they could save her life—[*Just help yourself to the sugar—*]

[POPEYE: (*Moving to sit on the floor.*) *Thanks.*]

CARNELLE: And they did, in fact, keep her alive for the month or so longer than she was expected to live.

[POPEYE: *Well that's good.*]

CARNELLE: (*Pouring herself some tea.*) Of course, there were such dreadful side effects.

[POPEYE: *Mmm.*]

CARNELLE: She, well, she started growing long, black hairs all over her body just, well, just like an ape

[POPEYE: *Gracious, Lord.*]

CARNELLE: It was very trying. But she was so brave. She even let them take photographs of her. Everyone said she was just a saint. A saint or an angel; one or the other.

[POPEYE: *It gives me the shivers.*]

CARNELLE: It was awfully hard on me losing my Aunt Ronelle—although I guess I should be used to it by now.

[POPEYE: *What's that?*]

CARNELLE: People dying. It seems like people've been dying practically all my life, in one way or another. First my mother passed when I was barely a year old. Then my daddy kinda drug me around with him till I was about nine and he couldn't stand me any longer; so he dropped me off to live with my Aunt Ronelle and Uncle George and their own two children: Elain and Delmount. They're incredible, those two. They're just my ideal. Anyhow, we're happy up until the time when Uncle George falls to his death trying to pull this bird's nest out from the chimney.

[POPEYE: *He fell off from the roof?*]

CARNELLE: That's right. Tommy Turner was passing by throwing the evening paper and he caught sight of the whole event. Boom.

[POPEYE: *How awful.*]

CARNELLE: Anyhow, my original daddy appears back here to live with us looking all kinda fat and swollen. And after staying on with us about two years, he suddenly drops dead in the summer's heat while running out to the Tropical Ice Cream truck. Heart failure, they said it was. Then this thing with Aunt Ronelle dying right before Christmas. It's been hard to bear.

MOONTEL SIX

Constance Congdon

The Play: Set on the Moon in the twenty-second century, *Moontel Six* tells the story of a colony of genetically altered teens (Meema, Zipper, Emo Seven, Toyn, and Geenoma) who leave the shelter of an abandoned motel in search of a home of their own—far from the reach of the residents of exclusive, gated Moonstead Estates who are set on their destruction. When the teens make their escape to Mother Earth, revelations are at hand . . .

Time and Place: The not-too-distant future. Earth's Moon and Earth.

The Scene: *Meema, a young genetically altered girl, recalls the moment of her birth and the most wonderful scientific discovery she has ever made.*

• • •

MEEMA: Well, I remember her. Her name was EF-#5783. Or "Jumba." She was thirteen years old. I lived in her womb for twenty-four months, so I grew to be a fairly large baby. I remember being inside. Lots of deep sounds came through me and they vibrated every cell in my body. I still try to make those sounds at night to comfort myself. But with my small lungs and elevated voice box, all I can manage is a medium tone, like singing. All it vibrates is my throat—not enough to lull me to sleep. When I was being born, I remember clearly being pushed along this tunnel towards a light. "Go to the light," I thought, but not in words because I didn't have any then. Then, suddenly, I was surrounded by light and I felt myself dropping, in a cloud, and, plomp, landing on the ground. It was a hard fall, but it bounced something out of this opening in my face. And then, wow! My chest expands and all this stuff comes in—like dry liquid it was. And then my chest collapses and that stuff goes out. And THEN I have to expand my chest myself because I need more of this dry liquid. And then, it goes out. And I'm breathing. That was breathing. And I still do it all the time without having to tell myself to do it! Now that seems like the most wonderful scientific discovery I've encountered so far. Breathing! And it even goes on when I'm asleep! And now, I'm on Earth, and I can breathe everywhere! I can run in any direction and never, never run out of oxygen!

NIGHTSWIM

Julia Jordan

The Play: This short one-act is a partial episode in the lives of two seventeen-year-old friends, Rosie and Christina. Late one night, Rosie appears at Christina's window and calls for her to join her in skinny-dipping.

Time and Place: The present at midnight; outside Christina's house.

The Scene: *Christina looks down from her window upon the awaiting Rosie and speaks of her fear at being caught swimming naked.*

• • •

CHRISTINA: They'll find our clothes again and they'll know they've got two naked girls again. And one will shine his flashlight on you and one will shine his flashlight on me. And the water that maybe was like swimming in black velvet when we were alone and moving will be cold when we're still and wondering what to do. And they will order us out and we will be naked and shivering and your tan skin will turn white and frightened. They'll see right into you. Your eyes will fix on them and you won't look at me. You won't tell me what to do and I'll be so cold. They'll say, "Come on out now, girls." And the water will fall away from your body with only hands and wrists, white elbows and arms to cover you. Your arms look so breakable. And I'll follow you watching the water run down your back. The flashlights will glare down our faces, down our legs. They'll shine their flashlights for each of us. They'll smile at us trying to cover ourselves. They'll hold our clothes above our heads and smile at us naked and say, "Jump." And you'll cry and I'll cry and I'll jump.

NONE OF THE ABOVE [1]

Jenny Lyn Bader

The Play: A romantic comedy, Jenny Lyn Bader's play *None of the Above*, tells the story of the relationship between Jamie, a spirited, upper-class private-school teenager, and her brilliant SAT tutor, who has worked himself up from a small town in rural New York. In the beginning, Clark regards Jamie as shallow and egocentric, and Jamie regards Clark as socially awkward and insensitive to her personal difficulties. Over a period of six months, though, tutor and pupil develop a relationship of understanding as they work to accomplish the goal of earning Jamie at least a 1600 on her SAT.

Time and Place: The present; Jamie's well-appointed Park Avenue room, New York City.

The Scene: *Clark has just accused Jamie of carelessly breaking an expensive vase and not taking responsibility for her action, to which Jamie defends herself.*

• • •

Jamie falls dead quiet. Then she bursts out, almost crying.

JAMIE: It wasn't me who broke the vase! OK? I didn't do it!
. . . I didn't break the vase. Someone else broke it and I took the blame. So please stop trying to fit me into your little theory of entitlement. Because I do *not* go smashing up precious antiques; that is not my idea of a fun time. I have never broken anything in my life.
. . . It was my boyfriend! Roger Auerbach. And I knew if I told them that he broke it they would make it a rule for me not to see him and it would be really tricky to violate that because they are like really good friends with the Auerbachs. And I thought I loved him. So I told them I broke it. That's

when they came up with the unique punishment of no allowance for thirteen years.

. . . He left me the following week for Sheila Martin. The nonentity who called the other day. The new girl in school. At this point everyone has been at Billington since nursery school and we usually don't take new people after seventh grade? So to have a new girl junior year is like a revelation. All of the men just melted. Also, she's richer than Donald Trump, and she buys him presents, which of course I had to stop doing when my funding was cut off. I have to discuss every potential purchase I make with my mother. So this cramps my style a little bit.

. . . Yeah, and if it weren't for the dealing I do? I wouldn't be able to afford the cabs. I'd be in dangerous neighborhoods. Alone. Dependent on the charity of insane adolescent men. The business itself is pretty dangerous. No one used to care, but now the mayor is cracking down on small-timers. We're living in a fascist state.

NONE OF THE ABOVE [2]

Jenny Lyn Bader

The Play: A romantic comedy, Jenny Lyn Bader's play *None of the Above*, tells the story of the relationship between Jamie, a spirited, upper-class private-school teenager, and her brilliant SAT tutor, who has worked himself up from a small town in rural New York. In the beginning, Clark regards Jamie as shallow and egocentric, and Jamie regards Clark as socially awkward and insensitive to her personal difficulties. Over a period of six months, though, tutor and pupil develop a relationship of understanding as they work to accomplish the goal of earning Jamie at least a 1600 on her SAT.

Time and Place: The present; Jamie's well-appointed Park Avenue room, New York City.

The Scene: *Clark has broken off the tutor/pupil relationship with Jamie. A couple of weeks have passed and Jamie is on the phone talking to her friend Justine about the situation.*

• • •

JAMIE: Justine. You're way too good for him. And it's definitely beneath your dignity to keep breaking into his e-mail account. *(Beat.)* No I haven't heard from him. *(Finds the contract.)* Oh, look, here's the contract he signed with my father. What was he thinking? Lawyers are such bad writers! I would get a D minus if I turned this in. "Wherewhichfore the party of the first part" . . . who are these schmucks? . . . "should Jamie Silver answer enough questions correctly to merit a 1600, thus . . ." *(Beat. Looking at the signature on the contract.)* You know another thing about Clark? He had terrible handwriting. I should have known he would leave. Just from his handwriting. *(Beat.)* Dr. Lorin says even though I'll never hear from Clark again I'll always have a part of him inside me.

What? No, I'm not pregnant! He meant—actually I have no fucking clue what he meant, but it seemed comforting at the time. *(Beat.)* I was thinking of going to this lecture at this New School. No I am not geeking out on you Justine. It's about probability. Chance. I think chance is cool. All right. Later. *(Hangs up, stares at the contract, reads to herself.)* "*Should Jamie Silver answer enough questions correctly to merit a 1600 . . .*" Should Jamie Silver answer enough questions correctly to *merit—(She freezes. Picks up the phone.)* Hi, is my dad there? Oh. Tell him to call me as soon as he gets back. *(She hangs up. The phone rings. She answers swiftly.)* Hello? Oh, hi Mrs. Hargraves. Maybe. I'd need to talk to her. Hi Peggy! What did you do this weekend? What did you buy? Oh I love Gaultier. How much was it? Tell me what you think the tax was. Estimate. Just follow your gut. Good! That was very close. Put your mom on. Mrs. Hargraves? I can work with Peggy. I charge a hundred an hour and I'd have to meet with her at least two hours a week if she's going to take the SAT in the next . . .

QUINT AND MISS JESSEL AT BLY [1]

Don Nigro

The Play: Henry James' ghostly novel *The Turn of the Screw* serves as the inspiration for this tale of how Quint, a valet, and Miss Jessel, a governess, from James' work became the phantoms of that story. Filled with tension and suspense, Nigro's play explores the dangerous relationship and rivalry that develops between the subservient Quint and the Master of Bly over their affections for the beautiful, headstrong, and troubled Miss Jessel. In the end, we have new insight into Quint and Miss Jessel, the ghosts who seem to stalk the orphaned Flora and Miles in *The Turn of the Screw.*

Time and Place: Mid-nineteenth-century England. Various locations in London and at Bly, a country house in Essex.

The Scene: *Miss Jessel sits alone in the residence in Harley Street, London, mending Flora's doll, from which Miles, Flora's brother, picked out the eyes. Miss Jessel recalls the beauty of Flora's mother.*

• • •

Sound of a ticking clock. Lights upon the wooden chair. Miss Jessel moves into the light and sits, holding a rag doll onto which she is sewing a button eye.

MISS JESSEL: Don't be sad, Flora, because Miles has torn the eyes off your dolly. Miss Jessel will sew on new eyes for her. The eyes, you know, Flora, are the windows of the soul. We use our eyes for important things like looking. It is with our eyes that we look in the mirror. And, of course, the girl we see in the mirror has eyes as well, and she looks back at us. She is our reflection and our double. She sees everything we do. She is like us, but she lives behind the looking glass and does the opposite of what we are. Sometimes I wish I could be her, live in her world. I know that she must be happy there, in the mirror, although sometimes she looks very sad. I think that when I am gone away, she will be here to take care of you, and she will look in the mirror and see somebody else looking back at her. When I look at you, I see your mother. Your mother was such a pretty girl. She and I used to sometimes sleep in the same bed, when we were little girls, and I would hold her in my arms and watch her sleep. And what do you see when you look in the mirror, my dear? A very pretty girl. A very pretty girl indeed, who will make all the men cry one day. So, Flora, remember, if men pluck out your eyes, just come to me, and I will sew them on again for you. I will sew them on again, so you can see. *(She finishes. Sits the doll on her lap, facing out. The button eyes of the doll look out into the darkness with Miss Jessel. The light fades on her and goes out.)*

QUINT AND MISS JESSEL AT BLY [2]

Don Nigro

The Play: Henry James' ghostly novel *The Turn of the Screw* serves as the inspiration for this tale of how Quint, a valet, and Miss Jessel, a governess, from James' work became the phantoms of that story. Filled with tension and suspense, Nigro's play explores the dangerous relationship and rivalry that develops between the subservient Quint and the Master of Bly over their affections for the beautiful, headstrong, and troubled Miss Jessel. In the end, we have new insight into Quint and Miss Jessel, the ghosts who seem to stalk the orphaned Flora and Miles in *The Turn of the Screw.*

Time and Place: Mid-nineteenth-century England. Various locations in London and at Bly, a country house in Essex.

The Scene: *Miss Jessel speaks of the bad dreams that upset her so much as a child.*

• • •

Sound of the clicking clock. Night. Lights up on Miss Jessel, sitting on a chair by a small lamp, holding the rag doll in her lap.

MISS JESSEL: It was only a bad dream, Flora, and we must not allow bad dreams to upset us too much. When I was a girl, I had many bad dreams. I dreamed something horrible lived under my bed and came up at night to creep under the covers and lie on top of me and smother me. I dreamed that something lived in the closet and the door would creak open at midnight and a hideous spider creature with two red eyes would look out at me. I dreamed that my father was dead and I crawled up into the coffin so I could be put in the tomb with him, and he reached up his cold, dead hand and stroked my hair. I dreamed that I sat naked and cold upon the top of a high tower, sobbing and sobbing for my beloved, who had abandoned me. I dreamed that I was lying at the bottom of a dark, cold body of water, like a mirror, naked and shuddering and lost there. I dreamed that a man crawled up the side of the house and in the window of my room at night to suck out my brains through a straw in my ear. But you see, Flora, what a happy and well-adjusted young woman I have grown up into. So, you must conquer your bad dreams, too. Because your dreams really can't hurt you, you know, as long as you always remember to make a great show of carefully nurturing your indifference. It is always desire that kills, my love. It is always desire that kills. *(She reaches over and turns out the lamp. Darkness.)*

ROCK SCISSORS PAPER

Deb Margolin

The Play: This very short one-woman piece, originally part of the Actors Theatre of Louisville 2002 festival, tells the tale of an eighteen-year-old girl's ill-fated family vacation, her drug-dealing brother, and her mother, a woman unable to look at life directly and face facts.

Time and Place: The present, a therapist's office.

The Scene: *A girl sits facing her unseen therapist, openly revealing the most intimate details of her life.*

• • •

A girl of eighteen is sitting in a chair, facing an unseen therapist, whose back is to the audience. She speaks even the most revealing lines without a hint of self-consciousness.

GIRL: Whatever my mother's looking for is always *behind* her. I've noticed that. It never fucking fails. Whatever she can't find is always where her ass is. I'm upstairs, and she's screaming where the hell is *whatever it is,* and I'm just like, Mom, turn around! Just turn around, Mom! They say mothers have eyes in the back of their heads—well, yeah, right! My mom has trouble with the two in front! Once she was like, I smell fire, and she's looking around sniffing, and the garbage can was on fire right where her butt was but she just never turned around.

We took this family vacation recently to Rapid City, South Dakota, which even the name Rapid City is pretty funny, and we tried to act like a family, only we all just based it on shows on TV. Trouble was, we all used different shows. For my mom it was like, Bill Cosby show, where the wife is some dignified doctor, for my dad it was *Home Improvement,* and for me it was like, *Roseanne.* So it was like three shows playing at once. Pretty bad. I wish my brother were still alive. I miss him bad. We fought like dogs but when he died it was like when a kid gets off the seesaw real fast without telling you and you're the one who's up in the air on the other side. I hate that he died. I just hate it. He once gave me this dirty picture, he said he got it from Joey diFlorio, this tough kid at school. It was really small, this picture, it was like, black and white and all, and my brother said it was a real picture of people doing it that Joey took himself, even though it was printed on like newspaper or something. Anyhow, I still have that picture, and it's like my brother whispering in my ear, laughing.

So there we are in Rapid City and my parents want to see Mount Rushmore, you know, that's that big rock or mountain or something with those men's heads carved into them. Movie stars, or whatnot. They had pictures of it all over the little dump we were staying in, and it just reminded me of those Siamese twins with one body and a whole bunch of different heads. Now that must be hell! But at least maybe one of them would have the sense to turn around and look at their collective ass if the garbage can was on fire! So my mother wants to go see this Siamese twin real bad, right, but I just wanted to be alone, I wanted to look at that picture, you know, maybe meet some like decent people my own age or something, right, so I said I just got my period and I wanted to stay in bed and maybe I'd meet them there later. They trooped off with their cameras and binoculars and Dad's Immodium pills and all that, and there I was by myself. It felt real good, but scary too, because I started remembering everything. Remembering stuff is like a burglar, you know what I mean? It just breaks in, even if you've got the door locked and you're like, sleeping or whatever. I got the picture out, and I remembered it like lying on my brother's desk where he used to cut his stuff. He had all these knives and like weird equipments he used to use to divide up the "fruits and vegetables," as he called it, and he bought all these sandwich bags and he had scales, and he weighed stuff on scales, and he "cut" it with different other stuff, like aspirin and just stuff around the house, and people used to come over all the time! And Mom just said, "God, he has a lot of friends!" This quickie-mart, right behind her back!

I put the picture back in my pocket, and I went downstairs. There was this cute guy with an earring in his nose, or I guess you're supposed to say a nose ring in his ear, or whatever, and he had a short shirt on and big cargo pants . . . kind of hot . . . and I was just not feeling normal because of thinking about my brother, so I put my finger across his stomach as I walked by him, and Jesus, was he shocked. I walked right out of that little dump and onto a trolley car of some kind to take me to the Siamese twin. Sure enough, there were my parents, standing in front of a glass wall, binoculars in hand, staring at those assholes carved into the mountain, and I thought of that game me and Kip used to play called Rock Scissors Paper, and I thought: if I could make that dirty picture bigger and put it over those assholes' heads, I'd win hands down, paper beats rock, paper always beats rock, it's just so endlessly cool, because in a way it makes no sense, but the rule still stands, it just stands, and you could tell my parents couldn't see the heads too well, they were squinting and adjusting their binoculars.

Funny thing was, the four heads, the idiots, were reflected perfectly well in the glass right behind them, and I just started laughing and crying, and I just started screaming, *Turn around Mom!* That's why they sent me here. *Turn around, Mom, just turn around!*

ROMEO AND JULIET
William Shakespeare

The Play: Perhaps the most famous of all love stories, *Romeo and Juliet* is a tragedy of character and circumstance. The "pair of star cross'd lovers" fall victim to family enmity between their feuding houses of Montague and Capulet, and the needlessness of their deaths brings woe to both sides.

Time and Place: 1595. Juliet's bedchamber.

The Scene: *In an attempt to reunite herself with her newly-wed husband, Romeo, Juliet acts upon a plan to feign death by taking a sleeping potion that Friar Lawrence has given to her.*

• • •

JULIET: Farewell! God knows when we shall meet again.
    I have a faint cold fear thrills through my veins
    That almost freezes up the heat of life.
    I'll call them back again to comfort me.
    Nurse!—What should she do here?
    My dismal scene I needs must act alone.
    Come, vial.
    (She takes out the vial.)
    What if this mixture do not work at all?
    Shall I be married then tomorrow morning?
    No, no, this shall forbid it. Lie thou there.
    (She lays down a dagger.)
    What if it be a poison which the Friar
    Subtly hath ministered to have me dead,
    Lest in this marriage he should be dishonored
    Because he married me before to Romeo?
    I fear it is; and yet methinks it should not,
    For he hath still been tried a holy man.

How if, when I am laid into the tomb,
I wake before the time that Romeo
Come to redeem me? There's a fearful point!
Shall I not then be stifled in the vault,
To whose foul mouth no healthsome air breathes in,
And there die strangled ere my Romeo comes?
Or, if I live, is it not very like,
The horrible conceit of death and night,
Together with the terror of the place —
As in a vault, an ancient receptacle,
Where for this many hundred years the bones
Of all my buried ancestors are packed;
Where bloody Tybalt, yet but green in earth,
Lies festering in his shroud; where, as they say,
At some hours in the night spirits resort —
Alack, alack, is it not like that I,
So early waking, what with loathsome smells,
And shrieks like mandrakes torn out of the earth,
That living mortals, hearing them, run mad —
O, if I wake, shall I not be distraught,
Environéd with all these hideous fears,
And madly play with my forefathers' joints,
And pluck the mangled Tybalt from his shroud,
And in this rage, with some great kinsman's bone
As with a club dash out my desperate brains?
O, look! Methinks I see my cousin's ghost
Seeking out Romeo, that did spit his body
Upon a rapier's point. Stay, Tybalt, stay!
Romeo, Romeo, Romeo! Here's drink—I drink to thee.
(She drinks and falls upon her bed, within the curtains.)

SAINT JOAN

George Bernard Shaw

The Play: One of Shaw's finest plays, *Saint Joan* led directly to the playwright being awarded the Nobel Prize in 1925. Unhappy with the way in which Joan had been treated by history, Shaw follows her life from its earliest stages through her leading of the troops at the siege of Orleans to her burning at the stake for heresy, and depicts a heroine who is at once proud, intolerant, naive, foolhardy and brave. Joan emerges as a realistic woman able to confront politics, religion, feminism, and creative evolution; she is a rebel for all times and places.

Time and Place: Fifteenth century, France

The Scene: *Joan is speaking with her loyal supporter, Jack Dunois. Now that she has achieved many successes and made Charles the real French King, the courtiers, knights, and churchmen are turning against her out of petty jealousy.*

• • •

JOAN: Jack: the world is too wicked for me. If the goddams and the Burgundians do not make an end of me, the French will. Only for my voices I should lose all heart. That is why I had to steal away to pray here alone after the coronation. I'll tell you something, Jack. It is in the bells I hear my voices. Not to-day, when they all rang: that was nothing but jangling. But here in this corner, where the bells come down from heaven, and the echoes linger, or in the fields, where they come from a distance through the quiet of the countryside, my voices are in them. *(The cathedral clock chimes the quarter.)* Hark! *(She becomes rapt.)* Do you hear? "Dear-child-of-God"; just what you said. At the half-hour they will say "Be-brave-go-on." At the three-quarters they will say "I-am-thy-help." But it is at the hour, when the great bell goes after "God-will-save-France": it is then that St. Margaret and St. Catherine and sometimes even the blessed Michael will say things that I cannot tell beforehand. Then, oh then —

SCHOOLGIRL FIGURE
Wendy MacLeod

The Play: Renee, an anorexic, and her best friend Patty, a bulimic, belong to a clique of popular high school girls driven by the urge to stay skinny. When it appears that the group's reigning queen will soon die (of anorexia), her dreamy boy-toy, The Bradley, is up for grabs—but only to the most petite girl in school. The ensuing power struggle takes Renee to new depths of trickery and Patty to new heights of self-discovery. As the competition heats up, the girls' actions are observed by The Tribunal, a Greek chorus made up of members of the media, famous anorexics, and long-dead friends prone to declaring such ultimatums as "Above an 8 is beyond the pale." As the schoolgirls battle it out for the perfect body and the perfect boyfriend, no one is left unmarked.

Time and Place: The present; an American high school and various locations.

The Scene: *In this closing monologue, Renee is at the moment of Perfection, as she is about to leave Patty, The Bradley, and her friends and life behind.*

• • •

Renee is left alone on stage. The lights go down to a single spotlight. Behind her we see a gurney being set up.

RENEE: No great loss. Patty will be happier in the Midwest— parkas camouflage a multitude of sins. And as for The Bradley, he wasn't really the prize, he was just the tacky little statuette. The prize is actually . . . well, true story. Back in the days when I had muscles, I would rent a patch of ice every morning before it was light and go out there and try to master my school figures. I would fiercely skate that figure eight, because down the pike the school figures would count for 40 percent of my Olympic score. I practiced them even when I was on land, waiting in line for the water fountain, pressing my sneakers into imaginary blades. I spent the wee hours of my pre-pubescence obsessed with the Russian judge's good opinion of my outside edge and do you know what happened? They did away with the school figure part of the competition. Just did away with it. Because nobody saw them. Nobody *wanted* to see them. The audience just cared about the part where a skinny girl wears a skimpy leopard trimmed with maribou and jumps around to a disco version of *Carmen*. What can we learn from this? I'm sorry . . . I forgot what I was going to say. Is it cold in here or is it just me? Oh, I know, what we have learned is that there is only so much in this world that we can control so by all means let us control what we can, achieve what we must. Perfection.

SECOND CLASS [1]

Bradley Slaight

The Play: Building on the delightful and often poignant *Class Action,* Brad Slaight's *Second Class* introduces us to such characters as Scott, a cyberspace Cyrano; Maggie and Herm, who communicate only through prerecorded tapes played on boom-boxes, and Andrew, who is tormented by his peers because of his scars. But these are only a few of the teens who take the audience into the travails of out-of-class encounters in high school.

Time and Place: The present. A modern high school.

The Scene: *Mirelle confronts that awful moment of truth when she must view her school photos.*

• • •

Mirelle enters holding a large envelope. She starts to open it and then seals it back closed.

MIRELLE: Thank God this is the last year I'm going to have to go through this. Some people just don't photograph well. I don't photograph well. But every year my mom insists that I get these stupid class pictures taken. She just doesn't understand. *(Starts to open envelope; quickly closes it.)* I can't look. They're gonna be awful. Just like every year. It wasn't so bad when I was in grade school. I mean, all kids are cute . . . in a kid kind of way. But lately, yikes! My Freshmen year I had "red-eye," you know, like cats have at night. Sophomore pictures would have been OK if the photographer hadn't caught me in "mid-blink" . . . I looked like I was stoned or something. Last year, I had a bad hair day. You think I'm making too much out of this? Well keep in mind that these pictures don't just sit in Aunt Bessie's drawer. They go right into the yearbook .

. . enshrined forever like a museum of frightening photos. Someone told me they use them on name-badges at class reunions . . . for the rest of our lives! *(Pause.)* Alright, there's only one way to do this. Like a pond of water. Dive right in. *(Pulls the proof sheet out and looks at photos; pause.)* Hey . . . these aren't bad. Not bad at all. I mean, I'm no "cover girl," but these are alright. Finally. Thank you, Jesus! I can live with these. *(Relieved laugh.)* I can live with these!

SECOND CLASS [2]

Bradley Slaight

The Play: Building on the delightful and often poignant *Class Action,* Brad Slaight's *Second Class* introduces us to such characters as Scott, a cyberspace Cyrano; Maggie and Herm, who communicate only through prerecorded tapes played on boom-boxes, and Andrew, who is tormented by his peers because of his scars. But these are only a few of the teens who take the audience into the travails of out-of-class encounters in high school.

Time and Place: The present. A modern high school.

The Scene: *Leaza tells of a painful day that she and her family will never forget.*

• • •

LEAZA: I was the one who found her. They say it's a miracle that I came home when I did. From the start I knew something wasn't right. Her car was parked kinda funny in the driveway. It was only 3:30 and she was supposed to be at work. Also, the front door was unlocked . . . that seemed pretty weird too. *(Pause.)* I heard the water running and normally I wouldn't have thought much of that, but it seemed so loud 'cause there was no TV on, no loud music, none of the things Haley usually did when she came home. The psychiatrist, Dr. Linda, told me that the fact the bathroom door was unlocked meant she wanted to be found. I'm not so sure about that. I opened the door and saw her there in the shower . . . sitting against the shower wall. She was still conscious but had lost a lot of blood. There was a note taped to the mirror . . . right above the razor blade. Didn't really say why, just that she was sorry and she loved all of us. *(Pause.)* Dad was really torn up about this, I think Mom was mostly embarrassed. She wanted us to keep it a family secret, but Dr. Linda set her straight about that. That something like this needs to be brought out and looked at from all angles. They say it will take Haley a long time to get over this and we all have to keep an eye on her, but not be too over protective. It's a fine line, they say. She may do it again, or maybe not. We all go to meetings a couple times a week. I don't think I can ever talk to Haley the way I used to. *(Pause.)* I was the one that found her.

SIX

Timothy Mason

The Play: A group of college students, taking part in a summer program to study the earth's ecosystem, encounter more than scientific and political issues. One among them may be an eco-terrorist.

Time and Place: The present in the isolated wilderness

The Scene: Selena (nineteen-twenty) tells the group of her lifelong connection to science.

• • •

SELENA: Science used to be so much fun. When I was a child it was this never-ending source of surprise, it was what play was for me, I lived in a continual state of "Look at this! Can you believe this? This is so amazing!" Hyper, hyper, thrilled, alive. I mean, "Will someone please medicate this child?" I was always. . . growing things on the kitchen counter, unpleasant green and black things in petri dishes, or plugging myself into the wall and flying across the room. The menagerie I had going in my mother's apartment, in the bedroom I shared with my sisters, crickets and salamanders and toads, and feeding my dear crickets, each of whom had a name and a history, to the salamanders and the toads, tears streaming down my face, thanking them, asking their forgiveness, saying good-bye and trying not to resent the toads or the salamanders because that was just their nature and if I didn't feed them my crickets, they'd die. Everything, when I was a kid growing up, everything rippling outwards, nothing unrelated to any other thing, falling in love with the earth, the earth, the immensity of it, the close motherliness of it, the totality. What a mistake, like falling in love with the damned English Patient, he's not gonna make it, people! It's sick and it's dying and it's we who are killing it and ourselves along with it and it all just gets wadded into a tight, lightless wad. I know, I'm preaching to the choir, screeching to the choir, really, but. Civilizations don't decline, they collapse. It took the Mayans ten years, just ten years to go from the height of their power and population to starvation, dissolution, dust. Vanished in an instant. So where are we on that scale? So close, so really incredibly close.

SMOKING LESSON [1]

Julia Jordan

The Play: This intensely evocative and poetic play portrays the story of several young girls who turn the violent death of one of their friends (Pearl) into a ritualistic religious observance. When Tom, a young man, who is implicated in Pearl's death, discovers the girls in the throws of their ritual, he is drawn in unaware that one of them knows much more about the death of Pearl than even he.

Time and Place: The present. Rural Mississippi.

The Scene: *Tom and the girls have been smoking, and teasing one girl in particular, Tare. Tare lets them know that she has special powers and fire at her fingertips.*

• • •

TARE: She didn't find me. I've always been here. Just 'cause you couldn't see me. Can't you see me at all?

. . . D'ij'ever think I was invisible because I wanted to be? Ever think of that?

. . . 'Cause I've got fire at my fingertips all right. I've got it all over me. I've got so much fire in my hands I've got to hold it tight so it won't burn you.

. . . I hafta hold it so tight you don't even know it's there. Ever think of that? Ever think I had so much fire I could burn you all down? You never did 'cause I can turn my fire into anything I want. Birthday candles and Roman candles, color fireworks to dazzle you. Campfires and bonfires and brushfires and wildfires and towering infernos. I can control it and I can do whatever I want with it. I've got all kinds of fire you can't see. I've got all kinds of fire at my fingertips. I've got fire all over me. I'm not afraid of fire. *(She takes the cigarette and presses the lit end into her palm, extinguishing it.)* We're two of a kind Tom Delaney. I've been watchin' you and we're two of a kind. Remember that.

SMOKING LESSON [2]

Julia Jordan

The Play: This intensely evocative and poetic play portrays the story of several young girls who turn the violent death of one of their friends (Pearl) into a ritualistic religious observance. When Tom, a young man, who is implicated in Pearl's death, discovers the girls in the throws of their ritual, he is drawn in unaware that one of them knows much more about the death of Pearl than even he.

Time and Place: The present. Rural Mississippi.

The Scene: *Tom has just accused Tare of spying on him and Pearl before her death.*

• • •

TARE: I was not spyin'!

. . . I don't hide on purpose. It just sorta comes natural to me.

. . . It's like the Indians.

. . . Like the American Indians. Maybe I've got some Indian blood in me. You know, like the Indians.

. . . Yeah, you know. Like they tell you in stories.

. . . Like when you're readin' in a story about how the Indians, before the Wild West. How the Indians . . . when it was really wild. How they could walk right through a forest or a valley or whatever, and not make a sound. Walk right through a forest in their moccasins or their bare feet, steppin' on twigs and leaves and all sorts of crackling things and not make a sound. Invisible 'cause no one would look for something they didn't hear. And they could stand so still the animals would just go about their business right in front of them. And not just squirrels, but foxes and deer and wolves even. I'm not that quiet. People don't hear as good as foxes and deer and wolves though. You probably know that. *(Tom looks confused. Tare gives him a moment to catch up.)* Well, I learned about it in the stories and and it sounded good. You know? Real good. So I tried it out. I got some Minnetonka moccasins. But I had better luck barefoot. I was born with leathery feet, so I've got all the equipment necessary, if you know what I mean. And I just tried it out. I was a kid and it was somethin' to do. Just walk softly and play Indian and I'm telling you, it's easy when you put your mind to it. You just think like your body's got water in the legs and you just pour that water slowly from one leg to the other. So slowly. And if you keep it smooth and still and not crashin' and sloshin' around, you're cool. If you keep it smooth it's silent. Easy, see? And you get to like the feeling of it. I liked it so much I did it all the time. Till I did it natural without even thinkin' about it sometimes. It's not sneaky. Spying sounds sneaky. It's not sneaky, it's quiet. It's hiding, but if you looked I'd be right there. If you listened, you'd hear me. You just didn't. You were busy being another way. You were too busy with Pearl to notice me.

SMOKING LESSON [3]
Julia Jordan

The Play: This intensely evocative and poetic play portrays the story of several young girls who turn the violent death of one of their friends (Pearl) into a ritualistic religious observance. When Tom, a young man, who is implicated in Pearl's death, discovers the girls in the throws of their ritual, he is drawn in unaware that one of them knows much more about the death of Pearl than even he.

Time and Place: The present. Rural Mississippi.

The Scene: *Tare tells Tom about having a "little something" of Pearl enter her when she touched her body.*

● ● ●

(Tare takes a deep breath.)

TARE: I *touched* her.
. . . Pearl. We three found her floating facedown in the water. My brain felt half asleep. I thought the water might wake me up. I felt it on my foot and I thought this water is touching her. The water touching me is touching Pearl. But I wanted to touch her for myself. I wanted to know what it was to touch. Mary Kate and Lisa Ann were screaming, just screaming and screaming. And I was in up to my waist then I just put my hand on her pretty neck. So soft and slippery. Just placed my hand there, not pushing or grabbing, just touching. No one's gonna believe me but you.
. . . And I felt somethin'! I felt this little something inside of her sit up and take notice. Just pop up and pay attention. And that little something, that little something, slipped into my fingertips, pulsed through my hand and ran up my arm. And I've got it inside of me. And I've been takin' care of it,

see? That little somethin', I think, was the eight-year-old part. And I've been lettin' it grow up with me 'cause it wanted to so bad. It couldn't just die 'cause her body did. It wanted to be fifteen so bad. Understand? Maybe it's just a memory, like a church thing, or maybe it's somethin' else, somethin' stronger. But it's somethin'. An active thing. Life left over, I think. And now it is. It is fifteen, that little somethin'. Both of us. Fifteen years old, inside and out.

THE SPIDER MEN
Ursula Rani Sarma

The Play: A story of an act of rebellion gone terribly wrong, *The Spider Men* concerns a group of Irish teens struggling for their own identity in a world filled with peer pressure and parental dominance.

Time and Place: The present. A campsite in the woods of rural Ireland.

The Scene: At the beginning of the play, a nose-ringed Sarah (fifteen), dressed in a school uniform and carrying a satchel, indicts her parents for their hum-drum ways.

• • •

SARAH: I got my nose pierced the day it happened. I'd wanted to have it done for ages but my mum said my dad would go insane, although to be honest I don't think he'd notice if I pierced both my eyebrows, my lip, my nose, my ears and got a tattoo that said slut across my forehead. Because he's not that kind of dad. He's the kind of dad that works all day and then comes home and sits in front of the telly and doesn't talk to anyone for the night kind of dad. It's like my mum threatens us with him just so we'll think he gives a shit but we know he doesn't. *(Beat.)* I read in a magazine about this girl who really wanted to get to know her parents, she turned fifteen and she wanted to form an 'adult relationship' with them but as far as I could see all that meant is that she wanted to talk about sex with them. I can't think of anything worse than having to talk about sex with my parents. It's disgusting. I mean when you talk about something, part of you is making little pictures in your head to go along with it even if you don't want it to. You know, like if I say to you, whatever you do. . . don't think of a pink elephant. *(Beat.)* What are you thinking of? *(Beat.)* See? So match that with talking about sex with your parents. *(Makes a face.)* It's just. . . disgusting.

TIME ON FIRE
Timothy Mason

The Play: In the words of the playwright: "*Time on Fire* follows the lives of a group of New England young people and a young British officer in 1775, each of them caught up in the turbulence of the American Revolutionary War. From the indentured farm laborer to the wealthy elite, from the runaway slaves to Quaker pacifists, no one escapes unscathed or unchanged. Adolescence is universally a time of upheaval, but when a young person's entire world is suddenly in revolt, there are no safe answers and personal choices have public consequences."

Time and Place: Summer of 1775 through Spring of 1776, East Haddam, Connecticut, and parts of Massachusetts.

The Scene: *Elizabeth Coles (seventeen), from one of the wealthiest families, and secretly a Loyalist, has befriended Epiphany Brown, a young Quaker girl. A young English spy has been captured, attempting to burn down the Brown home. Epiphany is conflicted—her passion dictates that she should be outraged by this act—her faith tells her that she must not condemn. Epiphany has been invited to Elizabeth's home to work on a quilt for the patriot soldiers.*

• • •

EPIPHANY: We don't kill. God forbids us to kill, so we don't. People call us Quakers/ We call ourselves Friends. It's hard on Tribulation, he's just a boy, revolution to him is an exciting word . . . I appreciate your kindness to me, Miss Coles . . . I think you know what I mean, Miss Coles. I think you know that East Haddam has become a less friendly place for my family and me in the past few months. We are distrusted now. People suspect us of being in sympathy with the British . . .

Miss Coles, I know what courage it must take to be seen with me in public, and to invite me to your home. I want you to know how much I admire you for it . . . I think of that poor boy they're about to hang, the one they call a British spy, locked up for months, not much older than Tribulation, so far from family and friends and anything he's ever known as home. And now, because he won't tell them whatever it is they want to know, he's to be hanged. I wonder, how did sympathy come to be a dangerous word? . . . All my life I have felt so much a part of things here. As though I were a part of the very earth of this town. As though I were made of the same stuff as the dust I walked on. The sound of the mill-stream was the sound of my own blood, running through my body. The air was my breath. I was home. That's what the word used to mean to me. Home was the place I was made of . . . Did that boy send himself? Do the patriot soldiers who will sleep under these quilts give themselves their own orders? I can't be too quick to give that boy or anyone else the name of "enemy." Perhaps I have enemies, I don't know. I know for certain that where I least expected a friend, I have found one . . . Friends are commanded to love. I must go . . . My name means "God appears to me." My brother is called Tribulation to remind us that in the midst of life we are in death. It's not always easy to be a Friend. You wish you had my heart, I wish I had yours.

WAR DADDY [1]

Jim Grimsley

The Play: *War Daddy* tells the story of two groups of orphaned teenagers drafted against their will into feuding militia groups in an unnamed war-torn country. One group travels with Eddie, the son of a famous general, General Potent; while the other group, led by General Handsome, aims to capture Potent's son and use him to barter for more power. As the teens fight for survival, they struggle to comprehend what it means to engage in a war that has raged for so long that no one remembers when it began, or why. When the two groups finally collide, the resolution is anything but expected. *War Daddy* examines what happens when future generations inherit the battles we begin, asking the question: What is the meaning of peace if it's something we have to kill for?

Time and Place: The future. A war-torn small town in a nameless country.

The Scene: *Fanny, a young girl, in the service of General Handsome, who has given up playing with dolls for carrying weapons, is often confused by the reasons people go to war.*

• • •

FANNY: I'm too old for dolls anymore. Now I have a gun and a knife. I had fun with the dolls. I had a doll that was a soldier and a doll that was a sailor. The soldier always beat up the sailor because that was what I thought should happen.

I have fun with the gun, too. My sister and I went into the army together, because it was that or go on the street begging or slaving yourself to somebody. I'd rather kill people, my sister said. Her name was Ellen. She was good to me, and she took me with her to the recruiter. We signed up for the recruitment camps.

She says we had more family than just the two of us but I think she was lying, I don't think there ever was anybody else. I know you're supposed to have a mother but I don't think I ever had one. Because I would remember if I did. No matter what my sister says.

Last time I saw my sister she had lost an arm. Her right one. She was having to learn how to do things with the left one, it was driving her crazy. She stepped on a mine, I think. Some kind of an explosion. I really don't know. I just kept staring at her while she was explaining, at the place where her arm used to be, and afterward I was embarrassed to ask what she had said.

Sometimes I pretend Poker is my sister. I don't tell her so, but she knows we're friends, she knows I like her. We hang together a lot; we always volunteer for the same details. It's good to have somebody you can be friendly with. I guess we're actually friends, but we don't talk about it. In General Handsome's army you don't talk about things like that, or people will get the idea you're soft.

When Mouth asks what's the price of freedom, I think about my sister's arm, and I think, well, that's pretty stupid, don't you think? Why would you want to be free without your arm? When Mouth asks why we fight, I think about having a mother, and I think we fight so in the future everybody can have a mother, and both arms, and then I think, well, a war is a pretty stupid way to make that happen, and then I get confused and sit down and clean my gun. I just clean it and get it ready till my questions go away.

I mean, I understand sometimes you need a gun, sometimes you have to fight people. Who could look at the world and not realize that? But I get tired of killing the people who can't fight back. I don't understand that part, really.

I met General Handsome once. She was not Handsome. She was really scary, I thought. But I'm really not that old anyway, what do I know?

WAR DADDY [2]

Jim Grimsley

The Play: *War Daddy* tells the story of two groups of orphaned teenagers drafted against their will into feuding militia groups in an unnamed war-torn country. One group travels with Eddie, the son of a famous general, General Potent; while the other group, led by General Handsome, aims to capture Potent's son and use him to barter for more power. As the teens fight for survival, they struggle to comprehend what it means to engage in a war that has raged for so long that no one remembers when it began, or why. When the two groups finally collide, the resolution is anything but expected. *War Daddy* examines what happens when future generations inherit the battles we begin, asking the question: What is the meaning of peace if it's something we have to kill for?

Time and Place: The Future. A war-torn small town in a nameless country.

The Scene: *Mouth, a young female soldier in Handsome's group, often speaks for the group and serves as leader, although she misses all the grown-ups who are no longer around to fulfill this role.*

• • •

MOUTH: Where I grew up there was plenty of everything. I come from a good family. My grandmother was still alive when I was little. I wasn't the only kid who still had a grandmother, either. We lived on a farm near a village where a lot of people settled to get away from the fighting. There was no fighting where we lived for a long, long time. We had it pretty nice, I guess.

We were the better sort of people, my mom let me know that. We were an old family and we owned the land we lived on. We had a big house and a lot of slaves to run it for us. Maybe you won't like my talking about the slaves like that, like we deserved them, but we never asked them to attach themselves to us, they just did. People who had nowhere else to go, nobody else to turn to, but us. So we took care of them. We put them to work in the fields and we helped them keep a bit of a roof over their heads and we looked after them. My dad used to say they were like our children, the slaves. We had a responsibility for them, we had to look after them.

People aren't all the same. There are people who understand how the world works and keep it working, and there are people who just stumble along letting bad things happen to them. There are people who are noble and good, like General Handsome, and there are the rest, the sheep, the slaves, the ones who end up in the camps. Even the ones serving in the army, I guess. They need people like me, to keep them in line, to keep them moving forward.

I always knew I'd be an officer in the army, since I come from the better sort of people to begin with. I'm young for an officer. That's because so many adults are dead now, even the people I grew up with. My mom and dad are dead because of General Burly. He gassed most of the countryside where we were living. I wasn't there at the time or I would have been dead, too. That's why I hate General Burly, that's why I'd do anything to hurt him.

General Handsome is a good person. I met her a long time ago, when she was friends with my aunt. I lived with my aunt after my folks died, and General Handsome came to visit. She was the most noble woman I had ever met. She was nice to me. I wanted to be like her. I still do.

If there's any hope for us, it's General Handsome. She's tough enough to do what's necessary to get rid of General Burly and the rest. People say she's ruthless but she has to be.

The world is a mess. You can't fix it by being virtuous and good. You have to be willing to do the hard things.

I've killed a lot of people, I've watched a lot of people die. I don't let myself get soft about it, there's no use in that. A lot more people will have to die before the war is over, before General Handsome wins. The quicker we get this over with, the better. So I go on doing my part. I even enjoy it a bit. There's no sin in that, is there?

Monologues
for
Young Men

. . .

A BIRD OF PREY

Jim Grimsley

The Play: A modern tragedy set in a large city in California where the young people face good and evil on their own terms, with calamitous consequences. Centering on seventeen-year-old Monty, who has just moved with his dysfunctional family from rural Louisiana to a complex urban environment, the play explores an individual's attempt to find personal faith, while struggling to shield loved ones from the temptations and dangers they encounter every day.

Time and Place: The 1990s. An unnamed city.

The Scene: *Monty and his friend Thacker, a smooth, cool, charming, world-wise boy in his late teens, have been talking about the value of prayer in protecting one's family. Thacker confides that he doesn't even know where his father is and how difficult his mother and he have had it since the father left.*

• • •

THACKER: I don't even know where my dad is, any more. Did I ever tell you that?

. . . That was a while back. I guess I was still in little kids' school. And for a long time we didn't have any money, my mom and me. It's just my mom and me. And we didn't have any money. Because he left us with this big house to pay for and these two cars. Mom still talks about that. *(Pause.)* I don't tell anybody about this stuff, much.

. . . First, she lost everything. The bank took the house and the cars, one at a time. Like torture, right? *(Pause.)* I was old enough to figure out what was going on. Old enough to look at Mom and know she was close to losing it. To going crazy, you know? Because she never handled money before, Dad did all that. She had a part-time job and she tried to go full-time but by the time she did we were living with my aunt, me and her in this bedroom with my aunt and uncle screaming at her to get her shit together. *(Pause.)* So I couldn't stand that and I started hanging out. You know. At the park, and other places. And I got into stuff. I learned how to make a little money in the park, and other places. *(Pause.)* Mom tried to stop me, to keep me at home, but I wouldn't do anything she said. It was like I hated her. I didn't. But it was like I did. So after a while she stopped, she let me do whatever I wanted. She acted like she didn't know I was staying out all night, or drunk, or whatever. *(Pause.)* We don't live with my aunt and uncle any more. We have this little apartment. I stay there most of the time. But sometimes I stay other places. *(Pause.)* I wish I could pray and feel better. I wish it could have helped me then.

THE ACTOR [1]
Horton Foote

The Play: In the midst of the Great American Depression (1932), a young man from Texas, Horace Robideaux, Jr., decides to follow his dream. Like the local minister who "heard a call" to preach, Horace experiences a like call—but his is to go upon the stage and become an actor. The conflict between what is expected of us and what we must do to fulfill our destiny is core to this poetic exploration by one of America's most celebrated playwrights.

Time and Place: Early Spring, 1932. Harrison, Texas.

The Scene: *Having recently won a prize for best actor at a state drama festival, Horace has earned the name "Rudolph Valentino" around school. Here Horace recollects when he first pondered what it means to receive a "call."*

• • •

HORACE: I've known for a long time too that's what I wanted to be. Since I was thirteen. You see I used to go for walks in the evening with my mother and daddy and we'd always pass on our walks Mr. Armstrong's house. I could always tell when we were approaching his house no matter how dark a night it was, because the fences around his house were covered with honeysuckle vines and you could smell the honeysuckle a block away. Anyway, Mr. Armstrong, a very old man, would always be sitting in the dark on his gallery and as we passed my daddy would always call out, "Good evening, Mr. Armstrong," and he would always answer, "Just fine, thank you. How are you?" even though my daddy had never asked how he was but only wished him a good evening, and my daddy explained to me that he always answered that way because he was deaf and couldn't hear what my daddy said and only imagined what he said, and then he would always add, "You know Mr. Armstrong was working in the cotton fields in Mississippi when he got a call to come to Texas to preach. And that's what he did. He came here to preach." I had never heard of anyone getting a call before to preach or anything else, so I asked my parents a lot of questions about getting a call. Could anyone get a call? They weren't sure about that since Mr. Armstrong was the only person they ever knew who actually had gotten a call. "Is that because he is a Baptist, is that why he got a call?" I asked. My mother said no, she had heard about Methodists and Episcopalians getting a call to preach although she hadn't met anyone personally that had except Mr. Armstrong.

. . . Anyway, a year later when I turned thirteen I got a call, just as sure as Mr. Armstrong did. Not to preach but to be an actor. I kept that to myself for a month and then I told Todd Lewis, who was my best friend before he had to move away, about it and he said if I wanted his advice I'd keep it to myself as people would think I was peculiar wanting to be something like that. And for good or bad I've never told anyone else. I asked my mother one time what she thought Mr. Armstrong did when he got his call and she said she couldn't be sure, but she imagined he fell on his knees in the cotton fields and prayed about it and listened to what God wanted him to do and God worked things out for him so he could come to Texas and preach, and that's what I did. I prayed about it and asked God what I should do and the very next year Miss Prather came here to teach fresh out of college, and she put on plays, and that was encouraging to me and I found out from my daddy where Mr. Dude Arthur's tent show would be in the next few weeks. He always had his itinerary because Mr. Arthur was a customer and often wrote my daddy to send him clothes while he was on the road with his tent show. He asked me why I wanted his address. I said just to write and tell him how much I liked his tent show and he said that was a good idea as Mr. Arthur and his brother Mickey were always very good customers, even though Mr. Arthur was often short of cash and had to have extended credit, since the tent show business was having hard times because of the movies. Anyway, I learned he was going to be in Tyler, Texas, in two weeks and I wrote him there, care of general delivery, which is what my father said I should do, and I reminded him in the letter who I was and that I sometimes waited on him in my father's store when he came to Harrison, and I would appreciate it if he wouldn't mention to anyone, not even my daddy, but the next time he was in Harrison, I would like very much to see him as I wanted to ask him how you go about being an actor. He never answered my letter, so I figured he had never gotten it. So last summer when he came here with his tent show, I went over to the boardinghouse where he stayed with his wife and brother Mickey, who plays all the juvenile parts in the tent show, and I told Mr. Arthur I had written him a letter, and had he gotten it. He was drunk and said he didn't remember my letter, what was it about. And I said I wanted advice as I wanted to be an actor. He said why in the name of God, and I said because I wanted to, and I believed I had a call to be one and he said, well, you're a fool if you think that and get over it. Mrs. Arthur came in then and said, "Dude, sober up! You have a show tonight," and I left.

THE ACTOR [2]
Horton Foote

The Play: In the midst of the Great American Depression (1932), a young man from Texas, Horace Robideaux, Jr., decides to follow his dream. Like the local minister who "heard a call" to preach, Horace experiences a like call—but his is to go upon the stage and become an actor. The conflict between what is expected of us and what we must do to fulfill our destiny is core to this poetic exploration by one of America's most celebrated playwrights.

Time and Place: Early Spring, 1932. Harrison, Texas.

The Scene: *Having gone to Houston to see a famous troupe of Shakespearean actors, Horace speaks of when he, himself, received the "call" to become an actor.*

• • •

HORACE: I never told my mother or my Houston grandmother I didn't see the Ben Greet Players and when they asked me what play of Shakespeare I had seen I said *Julius Caesar* because I had read that play in English class my junior year and I had memorized the "Friends, Romans, countrymen, lend me your ears" speech for the class, and I knew if they asked me questions about the play I could answer them. I didn't realize Adelaide Martin, one of my mother's friends, had gone into Houston that same day to see the Ben Greet Players and when she got back she called my mother to tell her about it and my mother said I had been there too and had liked it a lot, and Adelaide said she didn't care for it as she thought the Romeo and Juliet looked middle-aged and were too old for their parts. *"Romeo and Juliet,"* Mama said. "That's not what Horace saw," she said. "He saw *Julius Caesar.*" *"Julius Caesar?* Did he go to the matinee or the evening show?" Mother said to the matinee and Adelaide said that's the one she attended and there was no *Julius Caesar*, but *Romeo and Juliet*. When I got home from school my mother confronted me with this and I had to admit what I had done. She asked me what *The Shanghai Gesture* was about and I said it took place in a Shanghai brothel and that's all she had to know. She said I was deceitful and should be ashamed of myself going to a play like that. I guess I should have been, but I wasn't. All I could think about was how Florence Reed reacted when, as the madame of the brothel, she heard that her daughter, who she hadn't seen in years, turned up as one of the girls in the brothel.

(A pause. He sings again.)

"Once I built a railroad,

Made it run,

Made it run against time.

Once I built a railroad,

Now it's done,

Brother, can you spare a dime?"

I love to hear Russ Colombo sing that song. My father hates the song. He says it's too depressing. He says he likes positive songs like "Happy Days Are Here Again." He says the country needs to have songs like that so they'll be in an optimistic mood and not depressed all the time.

AFTER JULIET

Sharman Macdonald

The Play: What happens after the deaths of Romeo and Juliet? What happened to Rosaline, Romeo's first love? *After Juliet,* imaginative, powerful, and poetic, resonates with a contemporary take on love and death, war and peace, as Juliet's cousin, Rosaline, who also loved Romeo, struggles to cope with the aftermath of the lovers' deaths. The Montagues and the Capulets are experiencing a tense truce while the trial of those implicated in the deaths proceeds. To complicate the situation, Benvolio, Romeo's best friend, loves Rosaline and pursues her, but she will not return his attentions because he is an enemy to her family and she seeks revenge.

Time and Place: "This could be Verona. Or it could be Edinburgh, Dublin, New York or Liverpool. It could be 1500, 1900, 2000 or 3000."

The Scene: *Gianni, a witty sixteen-year-old boy of the Capulet family, muses to Lorenzo, another Capulet boy, about making a pot of tea.*

• • •

GIANNI: Tea. There is no point even trying to make it without first warming the pot. They do it. People do it. Lemon? Milk? They say, brandishing a cold tea pot. The question doesn't arise. Why? Why would you make tea if you hadn't warmed the pot. Once the pot's warmed, with boiling water mind. Once the tea's spooned in, dry and black and perfumed with bergamot. Not blended, no shred of dust. I won't have sweepings from the floor that some chap's relieved himself upon. Once boiling water is added. While waiting in that delicious pause when the tea is giving of its essence. Then the question of lemon or milk can be addressed. With Earl Grey lemon always. But in the winter I would maintain it has to be lemon any way. Whether Darjeeling or Assam; lemon and not milk in the winter. Because. There is always a danger that the milk is contaminated. Turnips. That's the danger. In the winter time. There are those who feed their cows turnips.

A.M. SUNDAY

Jerome Hairston

The Play: *a.m. Sunday,* which explores the tensions that permeate a biracial household, premiered at the Humana Festival of New American Plays in March 2002. The father, R.P., is African-American, and his wife, Helen, white. Their sons, Jay (fifteen) and Denny (eleven), suffer the consequences of their parents' difficult relationship. Each boy confronts individual interracial challenges among their peers as they attempt to overcome these obstacles. Jay is unable to openly date a girl from school (Lori) for fear of racial recriminations, and Denny struggles with labels of inferiority at school.

Time and Place: A.M. Sunday to Thursday morning. Early November. The home of R.P. and Helen. An urban setting. A bus stop. The woods.

The Scene: Wednesday. R.P. confronts his son, Jay, about who broke the family phone and why?

• • •

JAY: The phone wasn't working anyway, right? I mean it would ring. Ring and ring. But when me and Mom pick up, no one's ever there. I mean, who would do that? Can you explain it? I mean, if you can explain it, maybe that'll shed light on the whole thing.

   (Silence.)

I lied. It's not always silence. When the phone rings, and there's no one there. There was once, this one time when I heard something. This breathing. So I waited. To see if anything would be said. Was about to give up, but then I heard it. A voice. This uneven voice. One I never heard before, but still, somehow I knew she had the right number. And she asked me. She asked me this one thing. *(Pause.)* "Is your father happy?" *(Pause.)* I ain't say nothing. I stayed quiet. I stayed. So, she asks again. "Is your father happy?" And the way she said it. So desperate. Soft. Like she. Like she was in love with you. Or needed to be in love with you. Sounded in need of something. She asks again. And this time, I was about to answer, but once I got strength up to . . . she hung up. She hung up. I've tried making sense of it. But it's a mystery. A total mystery. But those sort of things happen, I guess. Mysteries go unexplained. Phones get broken. I don't know what else to say. I don't know.

THE AUTOMATA PIETÀ [1]
Constance Congdon

The Play: In a remote part of northern Arizona, a teen fashion doll named Bambi is tossed out of a car window by her feuding "mommies"—young sisters, Jennifer and Shambhala. Abandoned in the desert, Bambi falls victim to an illegal toxic waste dumping and, mysteriously, grows to human proportions. Along the way, she encounters a series of colorful characters, among them Norris, a young high school–age man; his sister, Maggie, a policewoman, and Vortexia, a large woman who speaks Spanish now and again, and Time, an ageless being. Mixed together, this play explores the meaning and non-meaning of life.

Time and Place: The year 2000, more or less. Northern Arizona, then New York City.

The Scene: *Norris and Maggie have been driving around in a bus looking for a place to call their own, when they pick up Vortexia. Thirsty and in need of a drink—should it be beer or a sprite—Vortexia's observation that beer is "an old part of civilization" sparks a diatribe from Norris.*

• • •

NORRIS: What civilization? From the Sumerians with that absurd cuneiform writing—what was all that about? And Mis-anni-padda, is King of Ur—what a name for a country? "Ur—I'm from Ur." What a name for a King! "Mis-anni-padda?" Sounds like some character on a stupid kid's show. And speaking of Urs—they lost the city of Agade—yes, it disappeared!! Sorry, everyone, particularly those of you with relatives in Agade, but, we lost it! We have no idea where it is? Yes, a city and it's gone. We thought it was there, and it's not, and we looked over there and it's not there, either.

And in Norway, they are carving pictograms on rocks, and what do you think it is? Stars to show them which way is South, so they could find their own stupid way out of there? No, it's some jerk on skis that a four-year-old kid could have drawn. And Egypt? They start regulating the sale of beer in 1500 B.C., heading off any problems with worldwide alcoholism, and, boy, didn't they clear *that* right up before it got started. And then the Germans started migrating—hold on to your pigs and your daughters and don't get them mixed up.

(To another driver.)

WHAT'S WRONG WITH YOU YOU MANIAC!!

And then some Greek names the strophe and antistrophe and didn't the world rest easy that night. What time is it? No problem! We got the water clock—some Assyrian invented one, so all his contemporaries could tell what time it is TO GO TO WAR which they did and did and did and still do—don't get me started. And Sappho, wrote her poetry-o, so women could have some art since only men were allowed in to see the Greek plays on the great White Way, in between getting pelted with pitch, sulfur, and charcoal, the beginnings of chemical warfare from the Spartans. Meanwhile, the Aztecs are throwing sacrificial victims down the two zillion stairs of their sun temples while gladiators are beating the literal crap out of each other to the delight of audiences who now have *their* own water clocks since some Roman re-invented the damn things. And the Chinese come to India—

Did you see that? PEOPLE THINK THEY OWN THE ROAD!!

—and the Japanese re-invent wrestling and London is founded by the Romans who have no right to be in Britain, but, what the hell—nobody has the right to be anywhere, except in Africa where we all started from the same small woman who, feeling decidedly unwell, laid down in some mud, staring up at the big yawning, uninterested sky, not knowing that she has already dropped a kid or two who will eventually be head of the African National Congress as well as driving this damn bus, wearing a big Band-Aid from skin cancer surgery because he's so white. But that was forty-thousand years ago, and we're already up to the year "one." Why "one"? You ask. Or not. Because all the calendars which didn't even have pictures of the Grand Tetons or cute kittens on them were deemed unsuitable because NOW—

Whoa!! This road is dark.

—we've got to number from the birth of various saviour types like Mithra and Buddha, but, who's kidding, it's JESUS who screwed up the counting—sorry, Maggie. And in North America, people are making mounds of snakes and pyramids and being very, very quiet so as not to wake up the huge mass of land filled with more and more unhappy, poor, desperate, not to mention, greedy and power-mad types who are fixing to be on the move again, like the Germans. And, speaking of which, the Visigoths invade Italy, alchemists look for the Elixir of Life, and Anglo-Saxons finally start wearing shirts. And some Chinese sailor named Tamo brings tea—get this—*from* India *to* China—China didn't have the stuff yet. And Theodoric gives King Gundebald of Burgundy—what? Yes, you got it, a water clock! Then a plague hits, starting in Constantinople and spreading everywhere, and there are disastrous earthquakes all over the world and, guess what? WE'RE ONLY UP TO 542 A.D.!!

THE AUTOMATA PIETÀ [2]

Constance Congdon

The Play: In a remote part of northern Arizona, a teen fashion doll named Bambi is tossed out of a car window by her feuding "mommies"—young sisters, Jennifer and Shambhala. Abandoned in the desert, Bambi falls victim to an illegal toxic waste dumping and, mysteriously, grows to human proportions. Along the way, she encounters a series of colorful characters, among them Norris, a young high school–age man; his sister, Maggie, a policewoman, and Vortexia, a large woman who speaks Spanish now and again, and Time, an ageless being. Mixed together, this play explores the meaning and non-meaning of life.

Time and Place: The year 2000, more or less. Northern Arizona, then New York City.

The Scene: *At the top of Part Two, the ageless being, Time, rails against the audience for ambling their way back into their seats.*

• • •

TIME: OK! We have a situation here. I can feel your hatred. Admit it! Everyone here has wanted to do me in, and in the most nonchalant fashion. "So, what are you doing hanging around?" "Oh, just killing —"
(Points to himself, with a vengeance.)
Oh no! You may be saying—"That's just an expression! We don't hate you, Time. You're a part of life. You heal all wounds and wound all heels." Well, I don't buy it! Not for one *moment*—every one of which I am, by the way. And isn't that the problem? I'm not just the boy at the valve at the reservoir that lets the water flow or not—I'm the water itself.

And you blame me, for death—of those you love—your pets, your friends, your family. And, finally, yourself.

But, at that last moment, you turn around and want more and more and more of me! You stand there, trembling, shaking the vessel of your life, hoping for one lasting drop—of *me*. And when that drop appears, you, every once in a while, breathe "thank you," but inevitably to some god or other. And then you gobble me hungrily down and belch up your death. And everybody left in the room hates me.

But I move on, because I MUST keep moving—and the wails of sorrow engulf me until my next step lands me in the birthing room. Oh, and *then* everybody loves me. They can't wait to hold on and remember every moment of me, even wanting to *stop me*. Or—when the baby gets older, and is a surly teenager, they want to go back—they want to *reverse me*.

They don't think about if the sperm could back up out of the egg whenever it wanted to, on some cosmic whine, like bad weather coming in—"Today, we have a cold front meeting a giant Cosmic Whim"—and, you're, like, sitting somewhere and wham! you suddenly start to shrink, undevelop, ungrow, simplify, until "whoosh," you're split back into an egg in your mother's womb and a sperm in your father's testicles. So, one moment you're here, the next moment—think of where your parents are right now—PING! You're back in their bodies!

And this is the most important thing—without me, everything would happen at once! You tired of Time's Arrow and its relentless constancy? OK—say good-bye to sequence, order, shape, sense, LIFE! So this is what I came to say. This is my elbow. Watch it as I walk out that door. Right. I'm outa here. And I'm not coming back until I am LOVED and NEEDED for who I am!

BABY WITH THE BATHWATER

Christopher Durang

The Play: This outrageous, witty, and satiric comedy, depicts the raising of a baby whom the parents have never checked the sex of. Presuming that the kid is a girl, they name it Daisy and raise "her" as such, only to discover later that she is a he. The resultant identity crisis of Daisy is the focus of the play, as she/he encounters a zany nanny, acts out a bizarre penchant for throwing him/herself in front of buses, and eventually confronts his/her sexuality before his/her analyst and stops wearing dresses.

Time and Place: Contemporary. The home of John and Helen.

The Scene: *Daisy comes before his/her analyst and discloses when he/she discovered she/he was a boy.*

• • •

DAISY: When I was eleven, I came across this medical book that had pictures in it, and I realized I looked more like a boy than a girl, but my mother had always wanted a girl or a best-seller, and I didn't want to disappoint her. But then some days, I don't know what gets into me, I would just feel like striking out at them. So I'd wait til she was having one of her crying fits, and I took the book to her—I was twelve now—and I said, "Have you ever seen this book? Are you totally insane? Why have you named me Daisy? Everyone else has always said I was a boy, what's the *matter* with you?" And she kept crying and she said something about Judith Krantz and something about being out of Shake-n-Bake chicken, and then she said, "I want to die"; and then she said, "*Perhaps* you're a boy, but we don't want to jump to any hasty conclusions," so why don't we just wait, and we'd see if I menstruated or not. And I asked her what that word meant, and she slapped me and washed my mouth out with soap. Then she apologized and hugged me, and said she was a bad mother. Then she washed *her* mouth out with soap. Then she tied me to the kitchen table and turned on all the gas jets, and said it would be just a little longer for the both of us. Then my father came home and he turned off the gas jets and untied me. Then when he asked if dinner was ready, she lay on the kitchen floor and wouldn't move, and he said, I guess not, and then he sort of crouched next to the refrigerator and tried to read a book, but I don't think he was really reading, because he never turned any of the pages. And then eventually, since nothing else seemed to be happening, I just went to bed.

(Fairly long pause.)

. . . Well I knew something was wrong with them. But then they meant well, and I felt that somewhere in all that, they actually cared for me—after all, she washed *her* mouth with soap too, and he untied me. And so I forgave them because they meant well. I tried to understand them. I felt sorry for them. I considered suicide.

BROKEN HALLELUJAH

Sharman Macdonald

The Play: During the longest siege of a city in American history, *Broken Hallelujah* is set in the smoky hollows of war-torn Petersburg, Virginia, where two girls have a life-altering encounter with one Confederate and two Union soldiers. Scottish playwright Macdonald explores the effects of the failing American Civil War on young soldiers and citizens in this new play, co-commissioned by A.C.T.'s Young Conservatory New Plays Program and Theatre Royal Bath. Rich in language and boldly truthful, *Broken Hallelujah* is a story of the effects of war on young people that is as timely as today's newspaper headlines. The young characters in this remarkable play have had little input in what ultimately will be their fate. Pawns in a decidedly adult conflict, the youth engaged in the siege of Petersburg must consider a future over which they have little control.

Time and Place: June, 1864 to April, 1865. Petersburg, Virginia.

The Scene: *Two Union soldiers sit around a campfire, awaiting battle. Stewart's been frying bacon and Hancock ponders where he's been and what's ahead.*

• • •

HANCOCK: Knew a man that cooked. Orderly. Used to be a butler. Mid battle this was. Cold Harbor maybe. They merge. They all merge . . . Ask me Grant's a butcher. Bring back McCLellan he didn't waste men's lives. Had the pack shot off me at Bull Run. Shell took the pack right off my back. Not a scratch on me. Not a scratch. Miracle they called it. I don't know though. See my hands. See them shaking. My hands think I've had my miracle. I've run out of miracles. Anyway this orderly, my friend the butler. Brass come in for lunch. He has chicken cooked, this orderly, the butler. Old chickens but chickens all the same. Don't know where he got them. He has potatoes cooked. And bread he has. All ready and laid out it is beneath the trees. Hot and savoury as a man could want. Battle makes you hungry. Never understood that. Men dying all around you. They can be friends even. You get hungry. All sorts of hungry. What do you think that is? What do you think? Brass sits down as well as they can. Aren't enough chairs so they sit on the grass some of them. Barrage starts up just as he's passing the butter, my friend the orderly. For the new baked bread. Shell near cuts him in half, butter in his hand. You'd think a man would die fast cut in two like that. He has time to look around him. See the state he's in. They left him there. They ate. And they savoured every last mouthful. In his honor. He was nice and fresh and dead see. You don't get that smell not when they're fresh. Buried him after. Proper bacon you got there. Good and proper. Look like you know what you're doing.

BURIED CHILD

Sam Shepard

The Play: Amidst the squalor of a decaying farm, a family harbors a deep-seated unhappiness that has led to destructive suppressed anger and violence—all born of a long-hidden secret. The drunken, ranting Dodge and Halie, his alcoholic wife, fight their way through each grim day, accompanied by their misbegotten sons, Tilden, a hulking ex-All-American football player, and Bradley, who has lost a leg in a chainsaw accident. When Vince, a grandson none of them recollects, enters their world with his girlfriend, Shelley, Tilden is compelled to unearth the family secret, and the possibility of redemption finally seems plausible.

Time and Place: A farmhouse.

The Scene: *Vince has just learned that he is to inherit his grandfather's farm, as dilapidated as it is. Now it's up to him to keep the line going. The night before, though, he had tried to run away, and Shelley asks, "What happened to you Vince? You just disappeared?" Bradley lies on the floor before them attempting to get his artificial leg, which Vince had kicked out of reach during an argument.*

• • •

VINCE: *(Pause, delivers speech front.)* I was gonna run last night. I was gonna run and keep right on running. I drove all night. Clear to the Iowa border. The old man's two bucks sitting right on the seat beside me. It never stopped raining the whole time. Never stopped once. I could see myself in the windshield. My face. My eyes. I studied my face. Studied everything about it. As though I was looking at another man. As though I could see his whole race behind him. Like a mummy's face. I saw him dead and alive at the same time. In the same breath. In the windshield, I watched him breathe as though he was frozen in time. And every breath marked him. Marked him forever without him knowing. And then his face changed. His face became his father's face. Same bones. Same eyes. Same nose. Same breath. And his father's face changed to his grandfather's face. And it went on like that. Changing. Clear on back to faces I'd never seen before but still recognized. Still recognized the bones underneath. The eyes. The breath. The mouth. I followed my family clear into Iowa. Every last one. Straight into the Corn Belt and further. Straight back as far as they'd take me. Then it all dissolved. Everything dissolved.

CELEBRATION
Tom Jones

The Play: In this allegorical tale, a young orphan travels to the home of the world's richest man, who has destroyed the garden of the Boy's orphanage. The Boy arrives during a magical New Year's Eve celebration. Among the curious revelers he encounters is a beautiful fallen Angel, who, before long, becomes the center of a ritualistic battle between Mr. Rich and the orphaned boy—each vying for her love. Ultimately, the youth overcomes his old, jaded opponent and rediscovers the promise of change and regains the lost garden of the orphanage.

Time and Place: Contemporary.

The Scene: *The Boy tells his story of why he's going to old Mr. Rich's house.*

• • •

BOY: You see, I'm an orphan. I worked inside the garden at the Orphanage. But then a funny thing began to happen. All of the people that I knew when I was younger began to disappear. At first I thought, "Oh well, they've all been adopted!" But then it wasn't just the other orphans. It was the teachers too. And the priests. Until finally there wasn't anybody left at all except me.—And then some men came with big machines, and they began to tear down all the buildings. They had a ball on a great long chain and they swung it—way, way out—above the trees and the garden. And then, when it came back, it smashed into the Face of God.
. . . Well, I ran over and I took the Eye of God—that was all that was left of the stained glass. Look, I'll show you!
(Gets "Eye of God" from his bag and holds it up. Music.)
I'm going to see the old man.

. . . He's having a party for New Year's Eve. I'm going to sneak in. I'm going to tell him what they did to the chapel. I'm going to make him stop tearing down buildings. We don't want a factory; we want a garden!

THE CURSE OF THE STARVING CLASS
Sam Shepard

The Play: The tale of a dysfunctional American family, the Tates, with enough food to keep from starving but not enough personal strength to fill the voids in other parts of their lives. The drunken dreamer of a father, Weston, and his burned-out wife, Ella, struggle to maintain their rundown family farm, but their search for freedom and security leads only to a bleak, empty future. Their precocious teenage daughter, Emma, rebels at the life with her family and meets a violent end, and her brother, the overly idealistic Wesley, unable to build the foundation his dreams require, is left with nothing more than a tortured vision of a cat tearing apart an eagle that has caught it in it talons.

Time and Place: 1978 (the present?); a small farm somewhere in the American West.

The Scene: *Wesley is cleaning up shards of wood from the door his father broke down the night before during a drunken outburst. As his mother fries him some bacon for breakfast, he recalls the images going through his mind as he lay in bed listening to the splintering of the door.*

• • •

WESLEY: *(As he throws wood into wheelbarrow.)* I was lying there on my back. I could smell the avocado blossoms. I could hear the coyotes. I could hear stock cars squealing down the street. I could feel myself in my bed in my room in this house in this town in this state in this country. I could feel this country close like it was part of my bones. I could feel the presence of all the people outside, at night, in the dark. Even sleeping people I could feel. Even all the sleeping animals. Dogs. Peacocks. Bulls. Even tractors sitting in the wetness, waiting for the sun to come up. I was looking straight up at the ceiling at all my model airplanes hanging by all their thin metal wires. Floating. Swaying very quietly like they were being blown by someone's breath. Cobwebs moving with them. Dust laying on their wings. Decals peeling off their wings. My P-39. My Messerschmitt. My Jap Zero. I could feel myself lying far below them on my bed like I was on the ocean and overhead they were on reconnaissance. Scouting me. Floating. Taking pictures of the enemy. Me, the enemy. I could feel the space around me like a big, black world. I listened like an animal. My listening was afraid. Afraid of sound. Tense. Like any second something could invade me. Some foreigner. Something indescribable. Then I heard the Packard coming up the hill. From a mile off I could tell it was the Packard by the sound of the valves. The lifters have a sound like nothing else. Then I could picture my dad driving it. Shifting unconsciously. Downshifting into second for the last pull up the hill. I could feel the headlights closing in. Cutting through the orchard. I could see the trees being lit one after the other by the lights, then going back to black. My heart was pounding. Just from my dad coming back. Then I heard him pull the brake. Lights go off. Key's turned off. Then a long silence. Him just sitting in the car. Just sitting. I picture him just sitting. What's he doing? Just sitting. Waiting to get out. Why's he waiting to get out? He's plastered and can't move. He's plastered and doesn't want to move. He's going to sleep there all night. He's slept there before. He's woken up with dew on the hood before. Freezing headache. Teeth covered with peanuts. Then I hear the door of the Packard open. A pop of metal. Dogs barking down the road. Door slams. Feet. Paper bag being tucked under one arm. Paper bag covering "Tiger Rose." Feet coming. Feet walking toward the door. Feet stopping. Heart pounding. Sound of door not opening. Foot kicking door. Man's voice. Dad's voice. Dad calling Mom. No answer. Foot kicking. Foot kicking harder. Wood splitting. Man's voice. In the night. Foot kicking hard through door.

One foot right through the door. Man cursing. Man going insane. Feet and hands tearing. Head smashing. Man yelling. Shoulder smashing. Whole body crashing. Woman screaming. Mom screaming. Mom screaming for police. Man throwing wood. Man throwing up. Mom calling cops. Dad crashing away. Back down driveway. Car door slamming. Ignition grinding. Wheels screaming. First gear grinding. Wheels screaming off down hill. Packard disappearing. Sound disappearing. No sound. No sight. Planes still hanging. Heart still pounding. No sound. Mom crying soft. Soft crying. Then no sound. Then softly crying. Then moving around through house. Then no moving. Then crying softly. Then stopping. Then, far off the freeway could be heard.

LA TURISTA

Sam Shepard

The Play: Taking its title from the "sickness" that can plague tourists in foreign lands where the water is not always fit for drinking, *La Turista* tells the bizarre tale of Salem and her partner, Kent. This unfortunate pair find themselves suffering from sunburn and la turista in a small hotel room in Mexico. Into their uncomfortable lives comes a filthy, precocious native shoeshine boy who vexes them until a witchdoctor and his son (who is dressed just like the boy) arrives to cure Kent of his malady. Later, Salem and Kent find themselves back in the States in another shabby hotel room in the Southwest, where Kent now suffers from a mysterious sleeping sickness and another doctor and son arrive—leading to additional ominous circumstances that border on the surreal.

Time and Place: 1968; a dingy hotel room in Mexico.

The Scene: *Shortly after the witchdoctor arrives, the boy, speaking directly to the audience, as if he is a tourist guide speaking to a tour group, provides the context of the region and the significance of witchdoctors.*

• • •

BOY: The people in this area speak the purest Mayan existing today. The language has changed only slightly since the days of the great Mayan civilization before the time of the conquest. It's even more pure than the Mayan spoken by the primitive Lacandones, who live in the state of Chiapas. It's even purer by far than the Mayan spoken in the Yucatan, where much Spanish and Ladino admixtures have been added. In short, it's very pure and nearly impossible for an outsider to learn, although many have tried.

. . . The man here is the most respected of all, or I should say, his profession is. But then, we can't separate a man from his profession, can we? Anyway, there are several witchdoctors for each tribe and they become this through inheritance only. In other words, no one is elected to be a witchdoctor. This would be impossible since there is so very much to learn and the only way to learn it is to be around a witchdoctor all the time. Therefore the witchdoctor's oldest son, whom you see here, will fall heir to his father's position. He listens carefully and watches closely to everything his father does and even helps out in part of the ceremony as you see here. A great kid.

. . . The people of the village are very superstitious and still believe in spirits possessing the body. They believe that in some way the evil spirits must be driven from the body in order for the body to become well again. This is why you see the witchdoctor beating the man. This is to drive the evil spirits out. The firecrackers are to scare them away. The incense smoke, or copal, as it's called here, is to send the prayers up to the god. They believe the smoke will carry the prayers to heaven. The candles are so that the god will look down and see the light and know that there's somebody praying down here, since the god only looks when something attracts his attention.

. . . Although there are several European doctors in town, the people will not go to them for help. Instead they call for the witchdoctor who comes to their home and prays for them and beats them up and then goes to the top of the mountain where the god of health is supposed to be. There is an idol there that the witchdoctor prays to in much the same way as you see here. Please don't try to go to the top of the mountain alone though, without a guide, because it can be very dangerous. Last year a group of students from an American university went up there and tried to steal the idol for an anthropological study and they were almost killed. It's perfectly safe with a guide though, and you can always find me in front of the pharmacy. Or just ask someone for Sebastian Smith.

. . . Of course, in the days before Christ, they used to sacrifice young girls to the gods. But now that's been made illegal by the government so the people use chickens instead. That's what the two chickens are for. They usually give the poor chicken a little drink of cane liquor to deaden the pain but sometimes they don't even bother. You'll notice a slight mixture of Catholic ritual incorporated into the pagan rites. This has become more and more apparent within the last century but the people still hold firmly to their primitive beliefs.

. . . The marriage is fixed by the family, and the partners have nothing to say in this matter. The girls begin having babies at the age of fourteen and usually have about fifteen children before they die. The average life expectancy is thirty-eight for women and forty-two for men. The women hold equal property rights as the men and get paid a salary by the men for each baby they have. The eldest son in each family always falls heir to the father's property. The puberty rites for boys are very stringent here and vary all the way from having the thumbnail on the right hand peeled away to having three small incisions made with a razor on the end of the penis. By the time the penis has healed they believe the boy has become a man.

(At this time, the Son takes all of Kent's clothes off except his underwear, and piles them neatly at his feet, while the Witchdoctor takes out his machete and waves it over the chicken. He also swings the coffee can back and forth and chants more intensely.)

. . . At this time the clothes are removed from the man in preparation for the sacrifice. The chickens will be decapitated and their bodies held over the man to allow the blood to drop onto his back. This will allow the good spirits to enter his body and make him well again. The clothes will be burned since it is believed that the evil spirits still reside in his clothes.

And if anyone should put them on they would have bad health for the rest of their days and die within two years.

. . . After this, the witchdoctor will pray over the heads of the chickens and then take them to the top of the mountain, where he will throw them into the fire and then do some more praying. Now is the time for the sacrifice. For those of you who aren't used to this sort of thing you may close your eyes and just listen, or else you could keep in mind that it's not a young girl but a dumb chicken.

MOONTEL SIX

Constance Congdon

The Play: Set on the Moon in the twenty-second century, *Moontel Six* tells the story of a colony of genetically altered teens (Meema, Zipper, Emo Seven, Toyn, and Geenoma) who leave the shelter of an abandoned motel in search of a home of their own—far from the reach of the residents of exclusive, gated Moonstead Estates who are set on their destruction. When the teens make their escape to Mother Earth, revelations are at hand . . .

Time and Place: The not-too-distant future. Earth's Moon and Earth.

The Scene: *Seven uses losing socks as a metaphor for understanding "how the world works."*

• • •

SEVEN: I'm going to help you understand how it happened. You see . . . when you lose one sock, it leaves behind its mate. Or partner. Let's call it "partner." So you wear the next pair and you lose one of those. Because it's actually more likely that you'll lose one of a matched pair than one of an unmatched pair because you rarely wear an unmatched pair because most people are less likely to wear and then wash the unmatched sock, unless they are us who have stopped washing them altogether, so the odds are even greater that the next sock to get lost will be part of a pair. Are you with me? . . . It's important, Meema. It's important to understand how the world works . . . Let's say you have ten complete, but distinct pairs of socks, meaning each pair differs from another, then it will be over 100 times more likely that the result will be the worst possible outcome . . . The Best Possible Outcome would be seven complete pairs left. Drawing two socks at random even from a drawer full of complete pairs is most likely to produce nothing but two odd socks. And, here's the interesting part—if you draw two socks at random from a drawer full of complete pairs of socks you are going to, probably, get two odd socks. . . . Facts make up the world, so probability is a religious experience. For me . . . you know what's really strange? The odds of two lost socks finding each other is astronomical, but to make pairs from a random collection of odd lost socks, well, that's unheard of. That's all I'm trying to say.

OLD WICKED SONGS

Jon Marans

The Play: After extensive playing engagements and touring, young piano prodigy Stephen Hoffman (twenty) is already burned out and jaded. While in Vienna he is sent to a Professor Josef Mashkan, a respected but "old school" teacher. Hoffman displays a sense of arrogance and resentment toward Mashkan because the old teacher is not really a piano virtuoso, but a voice teacher. The task is to explore the emotional depth of Schumann's song cycle "Dichterlieber" ("The Poet's Love"). As Hoffman unlocks the cycle, he rediscovers the passion he originally had for his art, and what it means to have empathy for others.

Time and Place: 1986; Vienna, Austria.

The Scene: *During the course of his lessons, Hoffman and his teacher have been arguing about how they can find common ground in their music, as singer and accompanist. The exchange opens up a recollection for the young musician of the time he visited the Nazi concentration camp at Dachau and the young woman he met along the way.*

• • •

STEPHEN: *(Serious again.)* Two weeks ago, I took the train to Munich. The next morning I took another train from Munich to Dachau—

. . . —I arrived at the station fairly early, assuming the ride would take a while. It took twenty minutes. Isn't that interesting? Only twenty minutes from the heart of Munich to Dachau.

. . . At first, I thought I was on the wrong train. So I turned to an older woman sitting next to me and asked her in German if this was the way to Dachau.

. . . And she said to me "I knew nothing that went on there!" From the train, I took a short bus ride to the camp. On the bus, a young woman in front of me turned around and said "What are you doing here?!" I told her, "I'm here to see Dachau." She asked me "why?" and I said *(Stammering.)* "because it's important for people to see this place." And she said, "but why do *you* want to see it?!" And I said: "because I'm Jewish." And then she said, *(Very casually.)* "well why didn't you say so in the first place?"

Then she told me to move over—and sat next to me. Her name was Sarah. She grew up in Israel. Her grandparents had been in Dachau. They didn't want her to see it. Together, she and I did.

It's funny. I was prepared for the "*Arbeit Macht Frei*" sign, the barbed wire fences, the guard posts. I wasn't prepared for how beautifully Dachau had been fixed up. No, covered over. Most of the buildings—gone. Those that were left—whitewashed. The grass—so green. A stream near the site of the camp had a quaint little bridge. If I hadn't known better, I'd never suspect theses few acres of land had been crowded with thousand of emaciated, tortured bodies.

There was a small museum which told "the story"— mostly through pictures. And under each picture, a description. The only problem—the descriptions were in German— *no* translations. So most people there couldn't read it since German was not the predominant language among visitors. For those of us who could read the captions, they supplied only the barest of facts. As I walked through, I was silent. Stunned. Feeling—numb from the experience. Not Sarah. She was enraged. I could see her whole body tightening up as we walked from room to room in the museum. Finally, we passed a guard and she started yelling at him, saying he was burying the truth! . . . And the whole time he just stood there expressionless—silent.

After that, we saw the crematorium. Sarah cried. I couldn't. I was too angry. And confused.

Before leaving, we saw the Israeli Memorial. It's a stone tower. You look into it by going down a ramp and peering through a gate. Inside, it's almost completely dark except for a small beam of light that shines down from the top . . . a single beam of light surrounded by darkness. You can't go inside the memorial. The gate's locked.

On the way out of the camp, we picked up a brochure—*this* one in English—telling us to "please stroll through the lovely *town* of Dachau after leaving." We didn't. For some reason, the Bavarian charm was lost on us.

That evening, we spent a quiet dinner together. At the end of the main course, Sarah asked if I would spend the night with her. Back at her hotel we made love. *(Surprised, embarrassed.)* It was hot. Really hot. For hours and hours into the night. And then again the next morning. And I kept thinking, "why is this so special? Because she's Jewish? Or because of what happened at Dachau? Or is she just great in bed? Or am I suddenly better in bed?" And then it hit me— *(Not pleased.)* You were right. That combination of sadness and joy. With one emotion heightened, so is the other.

The next afternoon, she caught her train to Prague.

And these last two weeks, I've wandered through Vienna, "the city of dreams." And every time I turned and saw a beautiful bridge or a quaint babbling brook, I broke into a sweat. And every time I got off the U-bahn and heard that recorded message, "End of the line, everybody off," I felt sick to my stomach. And thought of a man I had respected. Once. *(He starts to gather up his music.)*

THE PLAY ABOUT THE BABY

Edward Albee

The Play: As the Man says in *The Play About the Baby,* "If you have no wounds how can you know if you're alive? If you have no scar how do you know who you are? Have been? Can ever be?" Such is the central question in this dark, humorous, intelligent play that focuses on Girl and Boy, a beautiful young couple who give birth to a baby, only to have their perceptions about life shaken by the intrusion of the mysterious and sometime sinister Man and Woman who enter their life.

Time and Place: Today—anywhere.

The Scene: *Now that the baby is come, Boy is naturally very protective of his offspring. Who are this Man and Woman? Are they Gypsies? Gypsies steal babies!*

• • •

BOY: Gypsies steal Babies! You've never heard? It's famous; it's like the money scam. You don't know? The money scam? The Gypsy promises to double your money for you, so you bring it to her, or him, to be blessed, so it'll double, or whatever. You bring it in ten dollar bills, or something, in a big paper bag, and . . . the Gypsy puts the paper bag on the table, between the two of you, and the Gypsy blesses it, and starts chanting, or something, and the music starts, and the lights go all funny . . . and in the middle of all that the Gypsy pulls the famous switch . . . the famous switch of the bag. In all the chanting and the lights and the music and all, the Gypsy switches bags—takes *your* paper bag with all the money in it and puts another bag in its place filled with—what, I don't know—newspapers, or something, cut-up newspapers . . . the Gypsy tells you to bury the paper bag in your backyard without opening it and without anyone seeing you, and you're to leave it there for—what?—three weeks, so the magic can work, the money can double, or whatever . . . and you do it, because you're an asshole—you would have put your life savings in a paper bag and handed it to some damn Gypsy if you *weren't* an asshole in the first place. And so, after three weeks you go out and start digging up your backyard, since you've probably forgotten exactly where you've buried the paper bag with all your life savings in it, like the Gypsy told you to do. And your *husband,* who knows a lot more about gypsies than *you* do, is sitting down by now, his head in his hands, crying. And so you eventually find where you buried it, and you dig it up and you take it over to your husband to show him how the money's doubled, and you open up the bag . . . [and it's all cut-up newspaper] . . . and the Gypsy's probably in Miami Beach by now driving around in some snazzy convertible . . .

PLAYBOY OF THE WESTERN WORLD [1]
John M. Synge

The Play: In *The Playboy of the Western World* Christy Mahan, a shy Irish lad, who is hired on to clean pots in a small County Mayo pub, soon becomes the hero of the village when it is revealed that he has killed his tyrant Da. As a result, Christy gains the affections of the publican's fiery daughter, Pegeen Mike. When the old man shows up—not dead after all—there is much commotion that eventually leads to an understanding between Christy and his Da; but he leaves Pegeen out in the cold.

Time and Place: 1907. A pub in a village on a wild coast of County Mayo, Ireland.

The Scene: *Christy has been at his chores in the pub and talking with Pegeen. Up until the day he "killed" his Da, nobody paid him no mind. Pegeen, disappointed, says, "And I thinking you should have been living the like of a king of Norway . . ."*

• • •

CHRISTY: *(Laughing piteously.)* The like of a king, is it? And I after toiling, moiling, digging, dodging from the dawn till dusk with never a sight of joy or sport saving only when I'd be abroad in the dark night poaching rabbits on hills, for I was a devil to poach, God forgive me, *(Very naively.)* and I near got six months for going with a dung fork and stabbing a fish.
> [PEGEEN: And it's that you'd call sport, is it, to be abroad in the darkness with yourself alone?]

CHRISTY: I did, God help me, and there I'd be as happy as the sunshine of St. Martin's Day, watching the light passing the north or the patches of fog, till I'd hear a rabbit starting to screech and I'd go running in the furze. Then when I'd my full share I'd come walking down where you'd see the ducks and geese stretched sleeping on the highway of the road, and before I'd pass the dunghill, I'd hear himself snoring out, a loud lonesome snore he'd be making all times, the while he was sleeping, and he a man'd be raging all times, the while he was waking, like a gaudy officer you'd hear cursing and damning and swearing oaths.

[PEGEEN: *Providence and Mercy, spare us all!*]

CHRISTY: It's that you'd say surely if you seen him and he after drinking for weeks, rising up in the red dawn, or before it maybe, and going out into the yard as naked as an ash tree in the moon of May, and shying clods against the visage of the stars till he'd put the fear of death into the banbhs and the screeching sows.

PLAYBOY OF THE WESTERN WORLD [2]

John M. Synge

The Play: In *The Playboy of the Western World* Christy Mahan, a shy Irish lad, who is hired on to clean pots in a small County Mayo pub, soon becomes the hero of the village when it is revealed that he has killed his tyrant Da. As a result, Christy gains the affections of the publican's fiery daughter, Pegeen Mike. When the old man shows up—not dead after all—there is much commotion that eventually leads to an understanding between Christy and his Da; but he leaves Pegeen out in the cold.

Time and Place: 1907. A pub in a village on a wild coast of County Mayo, Ireland.

The Scene: *Christy, bright and cheerful, on a brilliant morning, holds a girl's boot in his hand, which he is cleaning.*

• • •

CHRISTY: *(To himself, counting jugs on dresser.)* Half a hundred beyond. Ten there. A score that's above. Eighty jugs. Six cups and a broken one. Two plates. A power of glasses. Bottles, a schoolmaster'd be hard set to count, and enough in them, I'm thinking, to drunken all the wealth and wisdom of the County Clare. *(He puts down the boot carefully.)* There's her boots now, nice and decent for her evening use, and isn't it grand brushes she has! *(He puts them down and goes by degrees to the looking glass.)* Well, this'd be a fine place to be my whole life talking out with swearing Christians, in place of my old dogs and cat, and I stalking around, smoking my pipe and drinking my fill, and never a day's work but drawing a cork an odd time, or wiping a glass, or rinsing out a shiny tumbler for a decent man. *(He takes the looking glass from the wall and puts it on the back of a chair; then sits down in front of it and begins washing his face.)* Didn't I know rightly I was handsome, though it was the divil's own mirror we had beyond, would twist a squint across an angel's brow; and I'll be growing fine from this day, the way I'll have a soft lovely skin on me and won't be the like of the clumsy young fellow to be ploughing all times in the earth and dung. *(He starts.)* Is she coming again? *(He looks out.)* Stranger girls. God help me, where'll I hide myself away and my long neck naked to this world. *(He looks out.)* I'd best go to the room maybe till I'm dressed again.

QUINT AND MISS JESSEL AT BLY [1]

Don Nigro

The Play: Henry James' ghostly novel *The Turn of the Screw* serves as the inspiration for this tale of how Quint, a valet, and Miss Jessel, a governess, from James' work became the phantoms of that story. Filled with tension and suspense, Nigro's play explores the dangerous relationship and rivalry that develops between the subservient Quint and the Master of Bly over their affections for the beautiful, headstrong, and troubled Miss Jessel. In the end, we have new insight into Quint and Miss Jessel, the ghosts who seem to stalk the orphaned Flora and Miles in *The Turn of the Screw.*

Time and Place: Mid-nineteenth-century England. Various locations in London and at Bly, a country house in Essex.

The Scene: *Quint sits on a chair, polishing a pair of boots and addressing the invisible Miles.*

• • •

Quint sits on a wooden chair, polishing a pair of boots, speaking downstage to the invisible Miles. The Master is still drinking in his chair, and Miss Jessel has seated herself upstage, also out of the light, doing a bit of needlepoint.

QUINT: Oh cheer up, young Master Miles. I know what it's like to be a boy. I do. You may not believe this, but I was a boy once, myself. Oh, yes. I can produce witnesses to verify this claim, if necessary. Even your uncle was a boy once. And in many respects, come to think of it, he still is. I lost my parents, too, at an early age. Mother was an actress and a part-time peach vendor. Father was a picture on the piano. Looked rather like Bonnie Prince Charlie, except of course he wasn't Scotch. Mother drank Scotch. She was a lovely woman, had many friends. She did more entertaining backstage than she did onstage. I remember as a small child listening to her entertaining the Prince of Wales behind a screen. That woman was talented. She could have sung grand opera. Your grandfather was a good friend of hers. In her last months, she grew uncharacteristically plump, rather like a Christmas turkey, cried a great deal, then took a midwinter dip in the Thames and sucked in rather too much cold water. Saw her in her coffin, perhaps her best performance, a wonderful still-ness, something she never managed to achieve in life. Hell is memory. But, lucky for me, your grandfather took me under his wing, brought me to Bly, made me a stable boy—oh, I could tell you such stories about horse shit—and then, in the course of time, his eldest son's valet. Your uncle. So I knew them both, your uncle and your father. And your mother. I was proud to serve them all. And now here I am with you. So, do you know what the moral of that sad story is, young Master Miles? The moral of that story is, having a dead mother may actually turn out to be a spot of good luck. So, cheer up, and tomorrow we'll go fishing in the lake. And if you're a very good boy, perhaps we'll use your little sister for bait. Won't that be fun? *(He spits on the boot and gives it one last bit of rather violent polishing as the light fades on him.)*

QUINT AND MISS JESSEL AT BLY [2]

Don Nigro

The Play: Henry James' ghostly novel *The Turn of the Screw* serves as the inspiration for this tale of how Quint, a valet, and Miss Jessel, a governess, from James' work became the phantoms of that story. Filled with tension and suspense, Nigro's play explores the dangerous relationship and rivalry that develops between the subservient Quint and the Master of Bly over their affections for the beautiful, headstrong, and troubled Miss Jessel. In the end, we have new insight into Quint and Miss Jessel, the ghosts who seem to stalk the orphaned Flora and Miles in *The Turn of the Screw*.

Time and Place: Mid-nineteenth-century England. Various locations in London and at Bly, a country house in Essex.

The Scene: *Quint tells Miles how to handle women.*

• • •

Lights up on Quint who sits down left in the merest sugges-tion of a small rowboat, fishing on the lake with a rather crude fishing pole, consisting of a piece of twine tied to the end of a cut branch and dangling into the darkness of the lake downstage before him, as Miss Jessel moves to the foot of the staircase and sits there in the dark, and the Master remains in his chair.

QUINT: Now, Miles, I know that women can be infuriating on occasion, but we must never lose our temper with our little sister, but always be gentle and patient with her, and make allowances for her, because when she grows up, she will be a woman, and women are not like us, or rather, while they are often not like us when we expect them to be like us, they are sometimes like us when we don't expect them to be like us, and sometimes they make us very, very happy, for perhaps as much as five or ten minutes at a stretch, and also very, very sad, for periods usually not exceeding sixty or seventy years at the most, and if we are very lucky little fellows, now and then they will agree to pretend to love us, through no inherent virtue of our own, at least for a time, while it's convenient for them, at any rate, and then, eventually, in the course of time, much like the black widow spider, they kill us and devour us. Unless of course we kill them first, but that is not playing fair, you see, Miles, because we are much bigger and stronger than they are, so we must, as a point of honor, allow them to murder us, unless of course we are members of the aristocracy, or at least have money, in which case we get to murder them. The important thing to remember about a woman, Miles, is that you must forget her and go on about your business, which is, unfortunately, entirely impossible. Oh, look. I believe I've actually caught something.

(The light fades on Quint as the Master finishes his drink, gets up, and disappears into the darkness.)

SECOND CLASS [1]
Bradley Slaight

The Play: Building on the delightful and often poignant *Class Action,* Brad Slaight's *Second Class* introduces us to such characters as Scott, a cyberspace Cyrano; Maggie and Herm, who communicate only through prerecorded tapes played on boom-boxes, and Andrew, who is tormented by his peers because of his scars. But these are only a few of the teens that take the audience into the travails of out-of-class encounters in high school.

Time and Place: The present. A modern high school.

The Scene: *Leon, a boy of Native-American descent speaks of his heritage.*

• • •

LEON: If you listen closely . . . you can hear the past. The voices of my ancestors. My people. *(Pause.)* Most of the kids here call me Leon, but my Indian name is Suyeta (Soo-yay-ta), which means "The Chosen One." I may not look it, but my father is part Cherokee, and my mother has some in her as well. They moved to this area right before I was to start school because they wanted me to be brought up on the land that once was the home of my people. Before the concrete and metal, before the malls and the mini-marts, this was all open space. My ancestral tribe lived, hunted, played, and dreamed on this very ground. *(Pause.)* One time I saw an Indian Warrior walking in this hall. His face was painted with bright colors, his clothes made of animal skin, his eyes burned with life. He turned and waved to me, as if to invite me on his journey. *(Pause.)* I don't talk much about this with my friends because they don't understand the ways of my people. They don't understand that my blood flows with such history. But in the quiet moments I feel near to those who came before me. And I have a connection to the past. Their spirit lives on. Even here. Even now.

(He thinks about that for a moment and then exits.)

SECOND CLASS [2]

Bradley Slaight

The Play: Building on the delightful and often poignant *Class Action*, Brad Slaight's *Second Class* introduces us to such characters as Scott, a cyberspace Cyrano; Maggie and Herm, who communicate only through prerecorded tapes played on boom-boxes, and Andrew, who is tormented by his peers because of his scars. But these are only a few of the teens that take the audience into the travails of out-of-class encounters in high school.

Time and Place: The present. A modern high school.

The Scene: *Marvin speaks of the violent world he hopes to escape.*

• • •

MARVIN: I spend a lot of time just hangin' in the halls, checkin' out some of the kids in the school. I start thinkin' about what it would be like to be them, to live their lives. And I wonder what it must be like to live in a house that has plenty of room. In a neighborhood where helicopters don't fly overhead all night long. I wonder what it would be like to have both a mom and a dad. To not worry about my little sister gettin' hit with a stray bullet because somebody's fightin' over a street they don't even own. To have my own bedroom where I have my own things that no one will mess with. To not have to watch my brother racing to the grave with a never-ending need for twenty dollar pieces of rock. And I wonder what it's like to go places—like the beach, another state, another country. To go somewhere . . . anywhere. To buy a pair of hundred dollar Nike basketball shoes instead of stealin' them. To not worry about the electricity bein' turned off, or the car bein' repo'ed. I wonder what it's like to have dreams instead of nightmares and to know that those dreams someday may actually come true. To look through brochures of colleges and universities and know that I have a choice. To see myself living long enough to become an adult. *(He watches several more students as they walk past him.)* And as I watch the lucky ones, I wonder most of all, what it would be like to have hope. To have just a little bit of hope.

(Marvin exits.)

SECOND CLASS [3]
Bradley Slaight

The Play: Building on the delightful and often poignant *Class Action,* Brad Slaight's *Second Class* introduces us to such characters as Scott, a cyberspace Cyrano; Maggie and Herm, who communicate only through prerecorded tapes played on boom-boxes, and Andrew, who is tormented by his peers because of his scars. But these are only a few of the teens that take the audience into the travails of out-of-class encounters in high school.

Time and Place: The present. A modern high school.

The Scene: *Mark finds himself in a most embarrassing situation during his S.A.T. exam.*

• • •

Mark sits on a cube; he is very intense.

MARK: Eleven o'clock in the morning. A cold sweat came over me as I looked down at my S.A.T. exam. All around me were hundreds of other nervous souls, completely at the mercy of this test. Like penguins stuck on a floating chunk of ice! The Test Monitors stood at the front of the room, with their roving surveillance-camera eyes, waiting to jump on anyone who happened to stretch their neck, or blink too many times. We couldn't move. We couldn't talk. We couldn't think. We could only hold these emotions inside. And then it started to happen. I began to feel a low, familiar rumbling deep inside my bowels. You see, I always get terrible gas when I'm nervous. And I was nervous plus over this test. Inside me was a gas-bubble the size of a beach ball, desperately trying to get out. Knocking with a heavy determined fist at my back door. Oh, I tried to suppress it, but it started to expand—the pressure was unbelievable. It got to the point where I didn't even dare shift my leg in fear that the corral gate would fly open. And the quiet, God was it quiet! Nothing to cover the impending sound; nothing that would allow me to let out some of the pressure. Then, without warning, the bubble pushed forward and exploded from me with an ear-splitting thundergust! A force so great it lifted me off my desk chair. That was followed by the sound of 312 snapping necks as they turned around to look at the source of this deafening blast. The Test Monitors' eyes dilated in angry disbelief. My fellow students faces twisted like cheap Halloween masks, as they tried to contain their laughter. That was the final straw. "Who are you to judge me?!" I screamed out loud. *(Pause.)* What happened to me that day quickly became legend. Go ahead and tell all you meet. I am not ashamed.

SIX

Timothy Mason

The Play: Isolated in the wilderness, six undergraduate students (Blair, Jessica, Danny, Alison, Maddie, Massemo) and their graduate assistant mentors (Adam and Selena) study the local environment and ecosystem. Along with learning about the five mass extinctions that have imperiled the Earth over the millennia, and of the threats that a sixth one may be not far off, they discover much about one another and themselves. All seems well until suspicions surface that one of their group, Massemo, is an imposter, perhaps an eco-terrorist. Is he, or will be become the group's hero?

Time and Place: The present; a wilderness area.

The Scene: *Massemo, a student not on the original roster for the project, has just shown up at camp on his own. Selena scolds him for having tramped through and contaminating part of their "old growth" study area. Before long, he is meeting some of the other students, who ask him where he's from.*

• • •

MASSEMO: I'm an Army brat, not my favorite expression, but there it is. Eventually, my dad? You can be a pretty high-up officer in the Armed Services and be drunk a lot of the time and get promoted and everything, but finally you're gonna get profoundly busted. And my mom fell in love with her pottery teacher, and I'm not prejudiced, I hope I'm not, but I just don't like her. My mom's pottery instructor. So I move around. I've got, my grandparents on my mom's side? I like them. They're just so terrifically happy when I visit them in Arizona and that's not something I always get from either of my parents, happy to see you, not judging you, whatever. That's where I just was, I spent a few months in the winter, spring, staying with my grandparents . . .

. . . I was staying in this senior citizen gated community in Mesa, Arizona—hey, Danny—where nobody should be living to begin with, nobody in that whole part of the country should be there because human beings tend to require water and there is no water there, it's the middle of the freaking desert and they pump the water in from places they shouldn't and suck water out of the aquifer and pretend there's nothing wrong with any of it, but The Circle of Palms Fifty-five and Over Gated Community is where my grandpa and grandma bought their retirement home and I'm not gonna beat them up about that because they're great and why shouldn't they be warm in winter, OK? And I really like swimming in their pool, so fuck me. You know Rodin's "The Thinker"?

. . . There's this figurine down there in Circle of Palms golf course that just captures it for me, just sums it all up. Because as we all know or should, the golf course is one of the single most potent killers of the earth on earth. So OK, in the middle of this course there's a little sculpture in the center of a cactus garden. Think "The Thinker": He's naked, he's sitting, his elbows on his knees, his chin in his hands. Right? OK, put a pair of Farrah slacks on him. Give him a red, short-sleeved Polo shirt. Put a little red golf cap on his head, spread his knees and stick a bag of golf clubs in there. He's not looking down and thinking, like "The Thinker," he's looking up and thinking. Looking up and off into the distance and he's thinking, he's wondering, he's pondering, as the creatures of earth die out forever, and the earth itself turns to dust. The wind. The lay. The lie. How do I play it? How?

. . . Selena. Come with me.

. . . *(To Adam.)*

Don't you touch her!

(To Selena.)

Anywhere, you name it, we live on earth, we are citizens of earth. There are no countries anymore, no flags, to hell with flags, we can go anywhere we want if we know that we truly belong everywhere.

. . . *(To Selena.)*

Come with me, *do* something.

(Including the others.)

You people, what are you doing? Moping? Life on earth is being savagely destroyed and *it makes me blue?* I don't have to do anything about it as long as I feel real bad about it? Pathetic! All of you, don't you ever get tired of being utterly useless? "I am a concerned citizen, I signed a petition about the rain forests," you're useless!

(To Selena.)

We're at war! We're losing! You're pretending it's not a war, you're pretending you're doing good by making a half-assed undergrad study of the forest!

THE STRAITS

Gregory Burke

The Play: *The Straits* refers to the Straits of Gibraltar and the chunk of rock that the British have been occupying for years to guard the gateway between the Atlantic Ocean and the Mediterranean Sea. Consigned to this rock we find four teenagers, Darren (fifteen) and an older sister, Tracy; "Doink," an unsettled kid who hopes to join the Marines one day—like his brother; and "Jock," an even more unsettled teen than "Doink." Set against the background of Britain's war with Argentina over the Faulkland Islands, the teens are keenly aware of the Spanish who inhabit Gibraltar, particularly "Doink," whose brother is in the thick of things there serving on HMS *Sheffield*. As the teens attempt to reconcile their life on Gibraltar with the lives of their Spanish neighbors, their bottled-up energies lead to sins that are all too human.

Time and Place: May, 1982. Gibraltar.

The Scene: *Jock and Doink have just been talking about what it must be like to kill someone. That's why Doink wants to join the Marines—to be in "proper combat" and kill the enemy. He recalls his granddad, who earned medals for fighting in World War II, and Jock tells of his granddad, who served as a Desert Rat in North Africa.*

• • •

JOCK: North Africa. That's where mine was. Desert Rat, he was. He got shot in the face once.

. . . Well, not shot. It was shrapnel from a shell. He was a despatch rider as he was ridin' his motorbike, yeah, this shell hits the road right in front of him, an' his bike an' him go straight in the fuckin' hole. He's lyin' in the hole an' his bike's fucked an' he's broke his arm an' a couple of ribs an' he says he can feel all his teeth are smashed and his mouth's full of blood. The shrapnel went in one cheek an' out the other. Took all his teeth out. He's lying there an' all of a sudden this big German jumps in beside him and my granddad's thinkin', fuck it I'm a goner, an' then the German fuckin' shrugs an' helps him up an' gets out a smoke and gives one to my grand-dad an' they sit there havin' a smoke an' a chat an' that. 'Cept he said he couldn't talk or smoke because he had this big fuckin' hole in his face. The German finishes his fag an' goes. So my granddad he sits there an' he thinks he better get a move on or he's gonna bleed to death. He climbs out the hole an' legs it till he finds some British an' they take him to hos-pital. The hospital stitched his face up but it made him look like he was smiling all the time cos they just pulled his cheeks back and stitched them together. An' they gave him this mas-sive set of falsers, yeah. So he looked like he was really happy all the time. He worked in a butcher's after that. No one knew a fuckin' word he was sayin'.

TIME ON FIRE [1]

Timothy Mason

The Play: In the words of the playwright: *"Time on Fire* follows the lives of a group of New England young people and a young British officer in 1775, each of them caught up in the turbulence of the American Revolutionary War. From the indentured farm laborer to the wealthy elite, from the runaway slaves to Quaker pacifists, no one escapes unscathed or unchanged. Adolescence is universally a time of upheaval, but when a young person's entire world is suddenly in revolt, there are no safe answers and personal choices have public consequences."

Time and Place: Summer of 1775 through Spring of 1776, East Haddam, Connecticut, and parts of Massachusetts.

The Scene: *When a young Quaker boy, Tribulation, tells soldiers from the Continental Army the whereabouts of a British soldier, he questions his sister, Epiphany, about his decision to do so.*

• • •

TRIBULATION: I did the right thing, didn't I?

. . . Did I do the right thing? I don't know if I did the right thing. And now they're treating me like a hero and I know it should feel good, but it doesn't.

. . . I needed God to tell me what to do this morning! Was God telling me to lock that man in and run for the militia, or was it just me doing it? When I tell myself it was God telling me, I feel I did the right thing. But maybe it just felt adventurous, finding the enemy soldier, to be the one who turned him in. I'm not allowed to go to war but I was the one who caught the redcoat. That felt good, it still feels good. And it doesn't feel like God.

. . . I tried talking to Father, Father gave me a dollar. You're the one I want to talk to. Sister, the man pounded on the door. He was sound asleep when I found him, I think I got the door shut before he saw my face, I hope so. I hope he didn't see my face, I pray to God he didn't see my face. I hope he thinks it was just some grown-up who caught him. He cried, Epiphany. After I got the door shut and barred, he pounded and he begged me to let him out. I never said a word. And then he started to cry, I could hear him. And I could have done it, I could have opened the door. He promised he would just go away, he wouldn't hurt anyone, he wouldn't set any more fires. He was hurt, he was tired and hungry. I could have lifted the bar and run. Nobody would have known. He could have walked out the door and into the woods. I could have had mercy on him, Epiphany, and I didn't.

(They're silent for a moment.)

(Continuing.) It's time to go to Meeting.

TIME ON FIRE [2]

Timothy Mason

The Play: In the words of the playwright: *"Time on Fire* follows the lives of a group of New England young people and a young British officer in 1775, each of them caught up in the turbulence of the American Revolutionary War. From the indentured farm laborer to the wealthy elite, from the runaway slaves to Quaker pacifists, no one escapes unscathed or unchanged. Adolescence is universally a time of upheaval, but when a young person's entire world is suddenly in revolt, there are no safe answers and personal choices have public consequences."

Time and Place: Summer of 1775 through Spring of 1776, East Haddam, Connecticut, and parts of Massachusetts.

The Scene: *The young British soldier, Winston, has been on the run from soldiers in the Continental Army. Cold and unwell, and nearly starved to death, he pauses to remember the friends he had and ponder what the future holds.*

• • •

WINSTON: Here is another letter I will not write or send. Friends. I try to remember your faces. Was one of you called Rebecca? I can't quite see any of you. There was a boy here of whom I grew quite fond, but I did not protect him as I promised. I did not know what it was like to be afraid. I know fear now, I have read that whole book with my skin.

I have run away from war. I left my friend the Drummer behind to die. I do not know where I am, but no one can find me here. Until I starve I will be safe.

The key is to be so quiet that Death won't know you are there. You don't move, you don't talk. You think very quietly if at all. I am thinking right now, but quietly.

They say that God sees everything but it can't be true, how could he bear to look? If His heart is merciful? He couldn't bear to see what happens to us, it would break His Heart. But Death never shuts his eyes, he never looks away. Death likes what he sees.

TYLER POKED TAYLOR

Lee Blessing

The Play: In this very short play that appeared as a part of *Snapshot,* an anthology of short plays at the Actors Theatre of Louisville, eighteen-year-old Loyal engages in erotic presidential fantasies on, what has become, an annual and ritualistic visit to Mt. Rushmore.

Time and Place: The present; at the foot of Mt. Rushmore.

The Scene: *Staring up at the visages of the great presidents on the face of Mt. Rushmore, Loyal stands alone on the observation deck, "muttering quietly, swiftly to himself—a kind of mantra."*

• • •

LOYAL: Tyler poked Taylor Fillmore pierced Buchanan Tyler poked Taylor Fillmore pierced Buchanan Tyler poked Taylor Fillmore pierced Buchanan Tyler poked Taylor Fillmore pierced Buchanan Tyler poked Taylor Fillmore pierced Buchanan—

(With sudden aggressiveness to someone on his right, unseen.)

What are you looking at? Back off. *Now.* There's plenty of room out here.

(Watching as the unseen person retreats, returning to his mantra.)

Tyler poked Taylor Fillmore pierced Buchanan Tyler poked Taylor—

(Suddenly to someone unseen on his left.)

Mom, can I have a little privacy? You and Dad just . . . find somewhere else, OK?

(Watching them move off, returning to his mantra.)

Fillmore pierced Buchanan Tyler poked Taylor Fillmore pierced—

(The mantra is transferred to house speakers and continues, very soft. As Loyal speaks live, it's as though we now hear his thoughts under the chanting.)

God, I wish I didn't live in Rapid City. Dad makes us come up here every year. "Someday you'll be president, Loyal." That's what Dad says, every damn year. "You'll be one of them. You'll be up on that mountain."

(With a furtive look at his parents, then staring up again.)

Washington was first. First in war, first in peace and first in my bedroom late at night. I dreamed of him deep in the woods, holding the dying General Braddock in his arms. He knew from that moment he would be a leader of men. I followed him for years. Lived in his billet, shined his boots, his sword. Watched him write by candlelight. And when he blew out the candle—My father in spirit, my teacher, my lover. I dressed him every morning, kissed him and watched him ride out through the cherry trees into battle. Jefferson when I got older. So handsome, so wise. I sat in his study, watching him write his correspondence. Every hour I'd remove a piece of my clothing. Finally he'd close his notebook. We'd make love all night. There were letters he wouldn't finish for days. I knew Lincoln before the beard—splitting rails with his shirt off. He'd gleam with sweat. So would I, just watching. I was a Rough Rider with Roosevelt on the Great Plains. All the men would sit outside in the frozen morning light, huddled over their coffee, while in the tent Teddy lay weeping in my arms, telling me about the asthma that stifled his childhood.

(Staring off to his left, toward his unseen parents.)

All right! I'm *coming!*

(The chanting stops. Loyal stares up again.)

I knew I was never going to be president. So instead I made love to them. Every year. Here. Staring up into their enormous, gentle eyes—wishing that one of them, any of them, all of them were my real father. Wishing I could

whisper into their ears the words I've saved for tonight—
when I'm finally eighteen, and here.

(A beat. He takes a deep breath.)

Tyler poked Taylor Fillmore pierced Buchanan Tyler poked
Taylor Fillmore pierced Buchanan Tyler poked Taylor Fillmore
pierced Buchanan Tyler poked . . .

(Slow fade to black.)

WAR DADDY [1]

Jim Grimsley

The Play: *War Daddy* tells the story of two groups of orphaned teenagers drafted against their will into feuding militia groups in an unnamed war-torn country. One group travels with Eddie, the son of a famous general, General Potent; while the other group, led by General Handsome, aims to capture Potent's son and use him to barter for more power. As the teens fight for survival, they struggle to comprehend what it means to engage in a war that has raged for so long that no one remembers when it began, or why. When the two groups finally collide, the resolution is anything but expected. *War Daddy* examines what happens when future generations inherit the battles we begin, asking the question: What is the meaning of peace if it's something we have to kill for?

Time and Place: The future. A war-torn small town in a nameless country.

The Scene: *Prick, "definitely a guy"; a member of General Handsome's army in pursuit of the other group of teens—a lover of war.*

• • •

PRICK: I don't like to talk. Some of the other jerks do, but I don't. We're all jerks in this squad except Mouth. Mouth gives the orders, Mouth knows the high commander personally. Mouth asked for volunteers for this mission and I was the first one to sign up.

Me, I like the killing part. Other people think the war should be over. I don't. I like the war. It gives me what I want. It gives me a gun. It gives me people to use it on. I'm strong because of the war. The war needs me, and I need it, and that's the way it is.

War all the time. War every day. That's the slogan. I heard it since I was a kid. My dad would say it. My granddad would say it. War all the time.

Why do we fight? All that crap. We talk about it all the time. You probably heard it already, us or some other dumb jerks. We fight to be free. The price of liberty is never free. Crap. If you have to kill to be free, what's free? It's crap, that's what. Killing's just killing. Plain as that. And that's who I am, the one with the gun. That's the only ambition I have.

You think you're better than me? You don't live here.

WAR DADDY [2]

Jim Grimsley

The Play: *War Daddy* tells the story of two groups of orphaned teenagers drafted against their will into feuding militia groups in an unnamed war-torn country. One group travels with Eddie, the son of a famous general, General Potent; while the other group, led by General Handsome, aims to capture Potent's son and use him to barter for more power. As the teens fight for survival, they struggle to comprehend what it means to engage in a war that has raged for so long that no one remembers when it began, or why. When the two groups finally collide, the resolution is anything but expected. *War Daddy* examines what happens when future generations inherit the battles we begin, asking the question: What is the meaning of peace if it's something we have to kill for?

Time and Place: The future. A war-torn small town in a nameless country.

The Scene: *Lazy, another one of General Handsome's squad—who says he's just like Prick, except he doesn't like to work so hard. He's tired of listening to Mouth, a female member and leader in their group who speaks for everyone.*

• • •

LAZY: I kill people because I like it. The other jerks in the squad think I'm lying. They think it's just talk, because I'm trying to copy Prick. But I really am just like Prick, only lazier. I like what we do, I like fighting in the army, and I wouldn't change a thing about it. I got no theories. But I got this difference with Prick, I don't like to work so hard.

The one I really want to shoot is Mouth. I think about that all the time. Sticking the barrel of my gun between those lips and shooting. Man, I'm so sick of hearing it day in and day out. I mean, I'm here, I'm in uniform, I'm doing my part for freedom and justice and the boss's bottom line, but I still have to hear this crap all the time. The individual is the atom of history. Even the smallest person's sacrifice can make a difference. We can win if we all pull together. Now is not the time to question our leaders. You're damn right it's not. Not while I'm out here waiting to get my ass blown up.

I mean, sure, I'm all right with killing people. But I'm not so all right with the idea that somebody might do the same to me. Prick doesn't seem to care, Prick acts like nothing can kill him. But I think I could die from cutting myself while I'm shaving, I think it's like that. That's the kind of stuff that goes on in my head that makes me not such a good killer, like Prick. I'm too worried that I might be the one to get it.

Mostly what I like to do is to lie around and think about stuff. Like dirty stuff. Or like what I want to eat. Or like what I would tell my dad if I ever saw him again. Or if I had a brother and sister, what that would be like. Mostly that's what I like to do, think about stuff.

WAR DADDY [3]

Jim Grimsley

The Play: *War Daddy* tells the story of two groups of orphaned teenagers drafted against their will into feuding militia groups in an unnamed war-torn country. One group travels with Eddie, the son of a famous general, General Potent; while the other group, led by General Handsome, aims to capture Potent's son and use him to barter for more power. As the teens fight for survival, they struggle to comprehend what it means to engage in a war that has raged for so long that no one remembers when it began, or why. When the two groups finally collide, the resolution is anything but expected. *War Daddy* examines what happens when future generations inherit the battles we begin, asking the question: What is the meaning of peace if it's something we have to kill for?

Time and Place: The future. A war-torn small town in a nameless country.

The Scene: *Nickel, another of Handsome's young soldiers, who's tired of being hungry all the time, and isn't worth a dime.*

• • •

NICKEL: My ma says she always called me nickel because I wasn't worth a dime. My ma was American, a nickel is American money, or it was. She got shot when General Potent invaded Handsomeland. He sent tanks and infantry through my town. Ma and me were living on the street, begging and stealing. Mostly stealing because begging didn't do much good any more, nobody had anything to share.

I can remember being hungry. Sometimes we had nothing to eat for so many days I lost track. These days we might skip a meal, sometimes; but that's nothing like what I used to go through. These days I get a little hungry on a march, but in those days, I would get hungry enough my stomach would knot into a marble right here, right in my gut, and even then I wouldn't get anything to eat.

We eat pretty good in the army. We eat a lot of beans and potted meat and bread that's usually pretty stale. Who knows the difference when you never get it fresh? You get used to stale bread after a while.

When we're on patrol like this we eat dry rations. It's like gnawing ropes with the flavor of meat. But I even like to eat that.

Give me a sweet any day. Give me candy or a nice piece of fresh fruit like we hardly ever get any more. Give me canned peaches or a bar of chocolate, and I'll shoot anybody you want me to. I'll shoot my own mother, who never wanted me to be in the army in the first place. I guess she wanted me to starve to death, like she did.

WAR DADDY [4]

Jim Grimsley

The Play: *War Daddy* tells the story of two groups of orphaned teenagers drafted against their will into feuding militia groups in an unnamed war-torn country. One group travels with Eddie, the son of a famous general, General Potent; while the other group, led by General Handsome, aims to capture Potent's son and use him to barter for more power. As the teens fight for survival, they struggle to comprehend what it means to engage in a war that has raged for so long that no one remembers when it began, or why. When the two groups finally collide, the resolution is anything but expected. *War Daddy* examines what happens when future generations inherit the battles we begin, asking the question: What is the meaning of peace if it's something we have to kill for?

Time and Place: The future. A war-torn small town in a nameless country.

The Scene: *Poker, a young guy and soldier for General Handsome, who wonders who started the war, and why?*

• • •

POKER: I grew up with a gun in my hand. I always knew I had to fight. My dad taught me how to shoot. We were in the backyard. I was a really little kid then, I didn't know anything. We had two rooms in a house, me and my dad and my mom and my sister.

I was just a little kid with the gun. I couldn't shoot it at first because it kicked too hard. It was a pistol, I don't even know what kind.

Where we lived was not in Handsomeland. We were under another general, I was too little to remember the name. Everything was quiet and peaceful and I went to school and learned my letters and numbers with all the rest of the kids and I had friends and enemies and we played together and then General Handsome came and bombed the school and killed most of the parents and put me in one of the recruit camps and because I knew my letters and numbers, I had to teach the other kids in the camp. My sister was there for a while and then they took her away. I never saw her after that. I still look for her sometimes, when I'm in a crowd. I wonder what she might look like.

We were happy and then General Handsome came and nobody was happy any more and now I'm fighting for him and I don't even know why. Except that's what people tell me I'm supposed to do, and that's all I hear. So they gave me this gun, and I have it, and I might as well use it to kill some people, since it's all such a mess out there anyway.

I wonder who started the war, and why? How long ago was it that the war began? I don't say any of this out loud, and I'm careful with my face so none of these jerks can tell what I'm thinking. Especially Mouth. I don't want Mouth to know I have any questions. Mouth knows the general personally, that's why he sent Mouth out to hunt for General Potent's son. So I keep quiet, I keep my questions to myself. But I still wonder, who started the war, why did it have to happen, and why couldn't anybody stop it once it started?

Song Lyrics as Monologues

. . .

In the Conservatory at American Conservatory Theater, we often explore song lyrics as spoken word in acting class. Song lyrics, especially by gifted poetic writers, offer a wonderful opportunity to deepen the actor's language skills. The canon of dramatic literature frequently requires the actor to artfully communicate heightened language, where the character speaks in poetic form. Although this is common in much classical drama, more and more contemporary playwrights are working in heightened language. Note the work of Tony Kushner, Constance Congdon, Cheryl Churchill, Mac Wellman, and others. Today's actors need to be skillful at communicating all kinds of language if they want to work on the many stages in this country.

Beyond using song lyrics in acting classes to sharpen language techniques, we have also produced full musical theater productions using contemporary composers' work to frame a journey seen through youthful eyes. Our repertory of new music theater work in this style has included: *Dangling Conversations: The Music of Simon and Garfunkle; Forever Young: The Music of Bob Dylan;* and *Ladies of the Canyon: The Music of Joni Mitchell.* In these productions (each produced in cooperation with the particular composer), the lyrics serve as the mode of communication. Much like a chamber opera, the collection of songs are stitched together and staged into a seamless performance, scene by scene (song by song), culminating in an interesting glance at the arch of the composer's body of work, refracted through the lens of the teen point of view. We found that their storytelling in song is universal and ageless. The lyric as a poetic form offered delicious opportunities to create characters and scenes. In fact, in rehearsals, we always began with the song as a monologue before we add music to the mix. Next, we've offered some of Dylan's lyrics for you to explore as monologues—speeches spoken by characters in need of particular intentions. We hope you too find the value in exploring the form and structure of a unique form of character communication.

LYRICS BY BOB DYLAN

BOB DYLAN'S DREAM

While riding on a train goin' west,
I fell asleep for to take my rest.
I dreamed a dream that made me sad,
Concerning myself and the first few friends I had.

With half-damp eyes I stared to the room
Where my friends and I spent many an afternoon,
Where we together weathered many a storm,
Laughin' and singin' till the early hours of the morn.

By the old wooden stove where our hats were hung,
Our words were told, our songs were sung,
Where we longed for nothin' and were quite satisfied
Talkin' and a-jokin' about the world outside.

With haunted hearts through the heat and cold,
We never thought we could ever get old.
We thought we could sit forever in fun
But our chances were really a million to one.

As easy it was to tell black from white,
It was all that easy to tell wrong from right.
And our choices were few and the thought never hit
That the one road we traveled would ever shatter and split.

How many a year has passed and gone,
And many a gamble has been lost and won,
And many a road taken by many a friend,
And each one I've never seen again.

I wish, I wish, I wish in vain,
That we could sit simply in that room again.
Ten thousand dollars at the drop of a hat,
I'd give it all gladly if our lives could be like that.

While riding on a train goin' west,
I fell asleep for to take my rest.
I dreamed a dream that made me sad,
Concerning myself and the first few friends I had.

A HARD RAIN'S A-GONNA FALL

Oh, where have you been, my blue-eyed son?
Oh, where have you been, my darling young one?
I've stumbled on the side of twelve misty mountains,
I've walked and I've crawled on six crooked highways,
I've stepped in the middle of seven sad forests,
I've been out in front of a dozen dead oceans,
I've been ten thousand miles in the mouth of a graveyard,
And it's a hard, and it's a hard, it's a hard, and it's a hard,
And it's a hard rain's a-gonna fall.

Oh, what did you see, my blue-eyed son?
Oh, what did you see, my darling young one?
I saw a newborn baby with wild wolves all around it
I saw a highway of diamonds with nobody on it,
I saw a black branch with blood that kept drippin',
I saw a room full of men with their hammers a-bleedin',
I saw a white ladder all covered with water,
I saw ten thousand talkers whose tongues were all broken,
I saw guns and sharp swords in the hands of young children,
And it's a hard, and it's a hard, it's a hard, it's a hard,
And it's a hard rain's a-gonna fall.

And what did you hear, my blue-eyed son?
And what did you hear, by darling young one?
I heard the sound of thunder, it roared out a warnin',
Heard the roar of a wave that could drown the whole world,
Heard one hundred drummers whose hands were a-blazin',
Heard ten thousand whisperin' and nobody listenin',
Heard one person starve, I heard many people laughin',
Heard the song of a poet who died in the gutter,
Heard the sound of a clown who cried in the alley,
And it's a hard, and it's a hard, it's a hard, it's a hard,
And it's a hard rain's a-gonna fall.

Oh, who did you meet, my blue-eyed son?
Who did you meet, my darling young one?
I met a young child beside a dead pony,
I met a white man who walked a black dog,
I met a young woman whose body was burning,
I met a young girl, she gave me a rainbow,
I met one man who was wounded in love,
I met another man who was wounded with hatred,
And it's a hard, it's a hard, it's a hard, it's a hard,
It's a hard rain's a-gonna fall.

Oh, what'll you do now, my blue-eyed son?
Oh, what'll you do now, my darling young one?
I'm a-goin' back out 'fore the rain starts a-fallin',
I'll walk to the depths of the deepest black forest,
Where the people are many and their hands are all empty,
Where the pellets of poison are flooding their waters,
Where the home in the valley meets the damp dirty prison,
Where the executioner's face is always well hidden,
Where hunger is ugly, where souls are forgotten,
Where black is the color, where none is the number,
And I'll tell it and think it and speak it and breathe it,
And reflect it from the mountain so all souls can see it,
Then I'll stand on the ocean until I start sinkin',
But I'll know my song well before I start singin',
And it's a hard, it's a hard, it's a hard, it's a hard,
It's a hard rain's a-gonna fall.
Yes, it's a hard rain's a-gonna fall.

CHIMES OF FREEDOM

Far between sundown's finish an' midnight's broken toll
We ducked inside the doorway, thunder crashing
As majestic bells of bolts struck shadows in the sounds
Seeming to be the chimes of freedom flashing
Flashing for the warriors whose strength is not to fight
Flashing for the refugees on the unarmed road of flight
An' for each an' ev'ry underdog soldier in the night
An' we gazed upon the chimes of freedom flashing.

In the city's melted furnace, unexpectedly we watched
With faces hidden while the walls were tightening
As the echo of the wedding bells before the blowin' rain
Dissolved into the bells of the lightning
Tolling for the rebel, tolling for the rake
Tolling for the luckless, the abandoned an' forsaked
Tolling for the outcast, burnin' constantly at stake
An' we gazed upon the chimes of freedom flashing.

Through the mad mystic hammering of the wild ripping hail
The sky cracked its poems in naked wonder
That the clinging of the church bells blew far into the breeze
Leaving only bells of lightning and its thunder
Striking for the gentle, striking for the kind
Striking for the guardians and protectors of the mind
An' the unpawned painter behind beyond his rightful time
An' we gazed upon the chimes of freedom flashing.

Through the wild cathedral evening the rain unraveled tales
For the disrobed faceless forms of no position
Tolling for the tongues with no place to bring their thoughts
All down in taken-for-granted situations
Tolling for the deaf an' blind, tolling for the mute
Tolling for the mistreated, mateless mother, the mistitled
prostitute

For the misdemeanor outlaw, chased an' cheated by pursuit
An' we gazed upon the chimes of freedom flashing.

Even though a cloud's white curtain in a far-off corner flashed
An' the hypnotic splattered mist was slowly lifting
Electric light still struck like arrows, fired but for the ones
Condemned to drift or else be kept from drifting
Tolling for the searching ones, on their speechless, seeking
trail
For the lonesome-hearted lovers with too personal a tale
An' for each unharmful, gentle soul misplaced inside a jail
An' we gazed upon the chimes of freedom flashing.

Starry-eyed an' laughing as I recall when we were caught
Trapped by no track of hours for they hanged suspended
As we listened one last time an' we watched with one last
look
Spellbound an' swallowed 'til the tolling ended
Tolling for the aching ones whose wounds cannot be nursed
For the countless confused, accused, misused, strung-out ones
an' worse
An' for every hung-up person in the whole wide universe
An' we gazed upon the chimes of freedom flashing.

THE ACTOR. ©2003 by Horton Foote. Reprinted by permission of Peter Hagan, The Gersh Agency, 41 Madison Ave., New York, NY 10010. Contact The Gersh Agency for performance rights.

A.M. SUNDAY. ©2002 by Jerome Hairston. Reprinted by permission of Ronald Gwiazda, Rosenstone/Wender, 38 E. 29th St., New York, NY 10016. The entire text has been published by Smith and Kraus in *Humana Festival 2002: The Complete Plays*. Contact Rosenstone/Wender for performance rights.

AFTER JULIET. © by Sharman Macdonald. Reprinted by permission of the author's agent. All inquiries should be directed to St John Donald, United Agents, 130 Shaftesbury Avenue, London WC2 England, 011-44 (207)166-5278, glewis@united agents.co.uk

THE AUTOMATA PIETÀ . ©2006 by Constance Congdon. Reprinted by permission of the author. For performance rights, contact the Joyce Ketay Agency, 630 9th Ave. #706, New York, NY 10036.

BABY WITH THE BATHWATER. ©1984 by Christopher Durang. Reprinted by permission of International Creative Management, Inc., 40 W. 57th st., New York, NY 10019. The entire text has been published in an acting edition by Dramatists Play Service (440 Park Ave. S., New York, NY 10016) which also handles performance rights.

BE AGGRESSIVE. ©2003 by Annie Weisman. Reprinted by permission of John Buzzetti, The Gersh Agency, 41 Madison Ave., New York, NY 10010. The entire text has been published by Dramatists Play Service (440 Park Ave. S., New York, NY 10016) which also handles performance rights.

A BIRD OF PREY. ©1997 by Jim Grimsley. Reprinted by permission of Peter Hagan, The Gersh Agency, 41 Madison Ave., New Your, NY 10010, who also handles performance rights.

BOB DYLAN'S DREAM. ©1963 by Warner Bros., Inc. Copyright renewed 1991 by Special Rider Music. All rights reserved. International copyright secured. Reprinted by permission of Special Rider Music, Box 860, New York, NY 10278.

BREATH, BOOM. ©2003 by Kia Corthron. Reprinted by permission of International Creative Management, 40 W. 57th St., New York, NY 10019. The entire text has been published in an acting edition by Dramatists Play Service (440 Park Ave. S., New York, NY 10016), which also handles performance rights.

BROKEN HALLELUJAH © by Sharman Macdonald. Reprinted by permission of the author's agent. All inquiries should be directed to St John Donald, United Agents, 130 Shaftesbury Avenue, London WC2 England, 011-44 (207)166-5278, glewis@united agents.co.uk

BURIED CHILD. ©1979, by Sam Shepard. Reprinted by permission of Judy Boals, Judy Boals, Inc., 307 W. 38th St. #812, New York, NY 10018. The entire text has been published in an acting edition by Dramatists Play Service (440 Park Ave. S., New York, NY 10016), which also handles performance rights.

CELEBRATION. ©1969 by Tom Jones. Copyright Renewed. Reprinted by permission of the author. For performance rights, contact Music Theatre International, 421 W. 54th St., New York, NY 10019.

CHANGES OF HEART. ©1999 by Stephen Wadsworth Zinsser. Reprinted by permission of Bret Adams Ltd., 448 W. 44th St., New York, NY 10036. The entire text has been published in an acting edition by Samuel French, Inc. (45 W. 25th St., New York, NY 10010), which also handles performance rights.

CHIMES OF FREEDOM. ©1964 by Warner Bros., Inc. Copyright renewed 1992 by Special Rider Music. Reprinted by permission of Special Rider Music. All rights reserved. International copyright secured.

CRUMBS FROM THE TABLE OF JOY. ©1998 by Lynn Nottage. Reprinted by permission of Peter Hagan, The Gersh Agency, 41 Madison Ave., New York, NY 10010. The entire text has been published in an acting edition by Dramatists Play Service (440 Park Ave. S., New York, NY 10016), which also handles performance rights.

CURSE OF THE STARVING CLASS. ©1976 by Sam Shepard. Copyright renewed. Reprinted by permission of Judy Boals, Judy Boals, Inc., 307 W. 38th St. #812, New York, NY 10019. The entire text has been published in an acting edition by Dramatists Play Service (440 Park Ave. S., New York, NY 10016) which also handles performance rights.

182

CRAIG SLAIGHT is the Director of the Young Conservatory at American Conservatory Theater. As both a director and an acting teacher, Slaight has worked passionately to provide a creative and dynamic place for young people to learn and grow in theater arts. With a particular commitment to expanding the body of dramatic literature available to young people, Slaight has published seven anthologies with Smith and Kraus Publishers, *Great Scenes from the Stage for Young Actors,* and *Great Scenes for Young Actors Volume II, Great Monologues for Young Actors, Great Scenes and Monologues for Children, Multicultural Scenes for Young Actors, Multicultural Monologues for Young Actors,* and *Short Plays for Young Actors,* coedited by A.C.T.'s Jack Sharrar. *Great Monologues for Young Actors, Multicultural Monologues for Young Actors,* and *Multicultural Scenes for Young Actors* were selected by the New York Public Library as Outstanding Books for the Teenage. Additionally, Slaight created the New Plays Program at A.C.T.'s Young Conservatory in 1989 with the mission to develop plays by professional playwrights that view the world through the eyes of the young. The first nine New Plays are collected in Smith and Kraus Publisher's *New Plays from A.C.T.'s Young Conservatory, Volumes I and II. Volume II* also received recognition from the New York Public Library as an Outstanding Book for the Teenage in 1997. Educated in Michigan in Theater and English, Slaight taught at the junior and senior high school, college, and university levels, prior to moving to Los Angeles, where he spent ten years as a professional director (directing such notables as Julie Harris, Linda Purl, Betty Garrett, Harold Gould, Patrick Duffey, and Robert Foxworth). Slaight is currently a member of the Artistic Team at A.C.T. and frequently serves on the directing staff with the professional company. In addition to the work at A.C.T., Slaight is a consultant to the Educational Theater Association, the National Foundation for Advancement in the Arts, and is a frequent guest artist, speaker, workshop leader, and adjudicator for festivals and conferences throughout the country. In August of 1994, Slaight received the President's Award from The Educational Theater Association for outstanding contributions to youth theater. In January of 1998 Carey Perloff chose Slaight to receive the first annual A.C.T. Artistic Director's Award. Slaight makes his home in San Francisco, California.

JACK SHARRAR is Director of Academic Affairs for the American Conservatory Theater, where he teaches in the M.F.A. program. He has served as a theater panelist for the National Foundation for Advancement of the Arts, has taught both university and secondary theater arts for over thirty years, and is a member of Actors' Equity Association and the Screen Actors Guild. His performance credits include roles at Michigan Repertory Theater, Mountainside Theater, the BoarsHead Theater, Theatre 40, Pioneer Theatre Company, A.C.T. studios, numerous media roles, and direction of over fifty plays and musicals. He is author of *Avery Hopwood, His Life and Plays* (UMI Press); contributor to Oxford University Press' *The American National Biography* and "The Gay and Lesbian Theatrical Heritage: A Biographical Dictionary of Major Figures in American Stage History in the Pre-Stonewall Era" (UMI Press); coeditor (with Craig Slaight) of numerous award-winning volumes of scenes and monologues for young actors published by Smith and Kraus, "Up In Avery's Room," a play; and "Avery Hopwood at 16: Second Thoughts on First Nights: The Diary of James Avery Hopwood, August 29–December 31, 1898." He has adapted Hopwood's *Far and Warmer; or, Tessie Steps Out!,* and F. Scott Fitzgerald's *The Debutante* (Playscripts, Inc.). He is a graduate of the University of Michigan and holds a Ph.D. in theater history and dramatic literature from the University of Utah.